"Reginald Ray is illuminating an essential point for our happiness, healing, and transformation in this priceless book. He clearly and profoundly shows us the importance of the spirituality of the body and how to practice in a way that can be integrated into everyday life. This is an eloquent expression of his work that has already helped many people."

—Anam Thubten, author of *Embracing Each Moment*
and *No Self, No Problem*

"*The Awakening Body* is an unusual book. It offers detailed somatic practices (meant to be accompanied by guided meditations offered online) for awakening to the vastness within—beyond thinking and conceptualization. As a Zen practitioner, much of this sounds familiar to me, but this practice is clearer and more detailed than typical suggestions offered in Zen. Reggie Ray has spent a lifetime working on somatic techniques, both in and out of Vajrayana Buddhism, and has distilled what he has learned into a concrete methodology. This book is of interest to those who would want to devote themselves to its practice—as well as those seeking illumination for their own meditation."

—Zoketsu Norman Fischer, Zen priest and poet,
co-author of *What Is Zen?: Plain Talk for a Beginner's Mind*

BOOKS BY REGINALD A. RAY

In the Presence of Masters: Wisdom from 30 Contemporary
  Tibetan Buddhist Teachers

Indestructible Truth: The Living Spirituality of Tibetan Buddhism

Secret of the Vajra World: The Tantric Buddhism of Tibet

The Tibetan Buddhism Reader

THE
AWAKENING
BODY

SOMATIC MEDITATION FOR
DISCOVERING OUR DEEPEST LIFE

Reginald A. Ray

 ▪ Shambhala ▪ Boulder ▪ 2016

Shambhala Publications, Inc.
4720 Walnut Street
Boulder, Colorado 80301
www.shambhala.com

9 8 7 6 5 4 3 2 1

First Edition
Printed in the United States of America

♾ This edition is printed on acid-free paper that meets the
American National Standards Institute Z39.48 Standard.

♻ This book was printed on 30% post-consumer recycled paper.
For more information please visit www.shambhala.com.

Distributed in the United States by Penguin Random House LLC
and in Canada by Random House of Canada Ltd

Designed by Greta D. Sibley

Library of Congress Cataloging-in-Publication Data
Names: Ray, Reginald A., author.
Title: The awakening body: somatic meditation for discovering our
    deepest life / Reginald A. Ray.
Description: First Edition. | Boulder: Shambhala, 2016. | Includes
    bibliographical references and index.
Identifiers: LCCN 2016010000 | ISBN 9781611803716 (pbk.: alk. paper)
Subjects: LCSH: Spiritual life—Tantric Buddhism. | Meditation—Tantric
    Buddhism. | Human body—Religious aspects—Tantric Buddhism. |
    Tantric Buddhism—Doctrines.
Classification: LCC BQ8938 .R337 2016 | DDC 294.3/422—dc23 LC
    record available at https://lccn.loc.gov/2016010000

FOR CAROLINE

CONTENTS

PART THREE

How the Practices Unfold

PART FOUR

Final Thoughts

THE AWAKENING BODY

INTRODUCTION

This book is about something that is not only beyond words: it is beyond thought. It is about our life, the individual life of each of us. It is not about the life we think we have or would like to have, the life we obsess about and talk to everyone incessantly about all the time; it is about something far more vast, mysterious, and unknown—the actual life that we are living moment by moment, the life that we can feel and sense, the ever expanding web of lived experience that is all of what we are, just now. We can't get our minds around this actual life of ours; all of our thinking cannot pin it down nor can any of our words describe or capture it.

At present, we do not really know this true life of ours; we do not know who or what we actually are; and so we approach our life from the wrong end of the stick, by trying to think about it and figure it out. But we are trying to fit something that is truly boundless into the grain of sand of our own conceptual capacities. Of course that can't work. No wonder we feel so much discomfort, dissatisfaction, anxiety, and pain in our life; no wonder we struggle

1

and struggle, and often seem never to get very much of anywhere. Try and try as we may, we can't contain the infinity and eternity of who we actually are in some neat little package of our thinking mind, no matter how sophisticated our thinking may be.

So we fall back on our habitual default and observe our life from the external standpoint of our conceptualizing, judging mind. When we do, it seems to be something we can stand apart from and look at, a quantifiable thing that we can label, categorize, and ruminate about. We can judge it, compare ourselves with others, and think well or poorly of ourselves depending on what we find. But in a way, we are caught in an endless loop that just keeps circling back on itself, with no exit: we sense this fragile body of ours; we are haunted by our more-or-less afflicted, uncertain, and unsatisfactory karmic situation with all its limitations; and though we try to make the best of it, basically we have a subtle or not-so-subtle feeling of being trapped in our own web. Seen from the outside viewpoint of our judging mind, this existence of ours seems quite circumscribed and small—rather paltry, petty, and insignificant. And it is certainly never really satisfying and fulfilling, at least not for very long.

But we could take another approach: we can look at our life from the inside. How would one do that? The first step is to realize that the mechanism of our logical, linear, linguistic mind may not be the only way of knowing something; it may not be the only way or even the best way to know ourselves or our life. "Knowing from the inside" involves setting aside the bright daylight world of the thinking mind and learning to view—to viscerally sense— our life from within the half-light of our body. In the imagery of the ancient masters of Chan Buddhism, we need to "take the great step backward" into the shadows, into the semidarkness of our body. We simply set our consciousness backward and down. And in that territory, the thinking mind is worse than useless; it is only going to get in the way.

We could look at it this way. There is map; and then there is territory. The map is the conceptual representation. It is the function of the left brain, thinking mind to create maps of our life, maps of who we are, maps of other people and the world, maps of the universe, maps of everything. But maps, as the saying goes, are not territory. The abstract, conceptual maps of our conceptualizing left brain are not—are worlds away from—the rugged, unknown terrain, the actual visceral territory of our lived experience. The mental map is a small and limited thing; the territory of the body goes on forever. When we set aside, temporarily, the maps and enter directly into the limitless domain of our body, we begin the amazing, unexpected journey of uncovering our deepest, most authentic being and our true life; and in the process, we discover the depths of being of the universe and our place within the whole. This is the hero's quest of old and here we are, people living in an apparently completely different age, about to embark on that very same journey.

Some people already possess the capacity to view life from within the body. But often in our modern culture, these people are precisely the ones who either go into hiding or suffer inordinately in the contemporary environment. They may not do well on standardized tests, and they could struggle with the expectations of competitiveness, aggression, and success that dominate contemporary societies and be viewed as outsiders. Often looked down on and marginalized, they may not have sufficient confidence in their experience or realize how important their ability is; they may not be aware of how essential this type of knowing is—to our individual selves and to the health of our culture and our world.

Those of us who do not possess much of this subtle, inward, somatic awareness will need some coaching and training. But everybody can learn it; it is part—perhaps the most important part—of our human inheritance. Although in modern culture this kind of knowing is not prioritized, to say the least, in other times and places, this knowing from the inside, knowing from within the penumbral space, is believed to be the most important of all things; it is seen as the only way to know anything completely as it actually is; it is regarded as the one thing that makes us truly and fully human.

As we gradually learn to see from within the body, we find ourselves in a limitless terrain, one that perhaps we did not even know existed. Most important, we begin to realize that the body knows experience in a very different way from our diurnal, digital, logical consciousness; the body beholds things directly; it has the capacity of what is called in Buddhism "direct perception," the ability to experience the phenomena of our life nakedly, without the overlay, the veils and cloaks, the filters and skewed interpretations of our thinking mind.

From within the body we realize how much of what we previously took for our self and our life wasn't real; it was little more than conceptual fabrication, made-up ideas, vapid abstractions, recycled assumptions, covering and essentially hiding our actual experience, our unique beingness, who we fundamentally are. We see that, in fact, we haven't been in touch with what is actually going on with our life; we have been living in a dream world of facsimile versions. This discovery can be shocking, but it can also be inspiring as it brings before us the real possibility of learning to see in a different way and of entering upon a journey of discovering our true life, the one that we currently do not know. What would it be like to experience our life directly, truly, and completely, to live it as it actually is? Before we die, wouldn't it be worth knowing this human existence of ours in its fullest possible measure and extent?

This may seem like a remote possibility, reserved for other kinds of people—mystics, poets, visionaries—in other times and places. Yet it is not so. In fact, this kind of nonconceptual perception, and the discoveries it opens up, can set in motion a fundamental human reorientation and transformation that perhaps we have always dimly suspected was possible within us, and that on some level we always deeply yearned for but didn't know how to engage.

But what I especially want to say is this: this kind of direct, nonconceptual knowing, the discoveries that burst forth from within it, and the journey it unlocks are entirely doable in our present, modern world in the life that each of us is now living. The somatic tradition in which I was trained, tantra or Vajrayana Buddhism, coming from Tibet, is all about discovering our true existence—which is lying in wait for us within our actual, present life—and making this most important and most fundamental of all human journeys. This somatic tradition was originally practiced in medieval India by laypeople with families, occupations, and all the worries and hassles—and the oppressions and indignities—of ordinary life; this same tradition, known as the indestructible path (Vajrayana) can show us how in this present world and in this specific life of ours, the deepest realization and fulfillment are not only possible but eminently possible.

In fact, the somatic teachings of this lineage are not just that realization in the midst of ordinary life is possible and doable; more than that, they hold that true enlightenment is *only* attainable by *not* separating ourselves and withdrawing from our life, our body, our emotions and relationships, from the totality of this rugged, gritty human incarnation of ours. Quite to the contrary, for this lineage, the only way to reach complete realization is in and through our completely embodied human existence.

In other words, our spiritual journey occurs not in spite of the ambiguous and problematic experience of our actual life but because of it. The journey begins with discovering this embedded, concrete existence of ours and then learning how to inhabit it fully and thoroughly; realization involves letting go of the last shred of our resistance to and separation from the concrete truth, the reality and "isness," of our actual life. And after that? In the following pages we can talk about (and will talk about) what happens next; but basically, you have to see it for yourself. For that reason, in this book and its practices, the experiential element will be emphasized strongly.

Because most of us are more-or-less alienated from our actual life and largely ignorant of it, we are going to need clear, accessible, and effective methods of transformation, bringing our awareness from the superficial, imaginary life we are now largely living and guiding that awareness down into the depths of our actual body and our actual life, here and now. Such methods—which are invariably meditational in nature, with their various kinds of mindfulness and awareness practices—have always been the strong point of the somatic Vajrayana traditions. In our lineage, we call this body of teaching "somatic spirituality"—that is, the spirituality of the body.

PART ONE

Somatic Spirituality

1

Somatic Meditation

The *Awakening Body* is about the practice of meditation when it is approached as an essentially somatic discipline—that is, when the body rather than the mind becomes the fundamental arena of meditation practice. What might it mean to engage in this type of "Somatic Meditation"? Most simply put, rather than trying to develop meditation through our left brain, thinking mind in a "top-down" manner, as is the case with most contemporary approaches, Somatic Meditation involves a bottom-up process; in this bottom-up approach, we are able to connect with the inherent, self-existing wakefulness *that is already present within the body itself.* In contrast to contrived, conventional approaches that emphasize entry into the meditative state through the intentional thinking of the conscious mind and by following conceptual instructional templates, maps, and techniques, Somatic Meditation develops a meditative consciousness that is accessed through the spontaneous feelings, sensations, visceral intuitions, and felt senses of the body itself. We are simply trying to tune in to the basic awareness of the body. Put in the language of Buddhism, the human body, as such, is already and always abiding in the meditative state, the domain of awakening—and we are just trying to gain entry into that.

Since the kind of meditation I want to teach you in this book is in many respects quite different from what is conventionally understood as "meditation" in our modern culture, I want to say a little more about it. Meditation approached as a somatic practice involves two aspects. The first involves paying attention to our body, bringing our conscious intention and focus to and into our physical form. Sometimes we pay attention to individual parts of our body, even very minute parts; other times, what we are attending to is our body—or our "Soma," as I prefer to call it—as a whole. Sometimes our attention will be on physical sensations, other times on body-wide events and patterns, others again on the subtle energies that flow through our body, other times the spatial environment of our body, other times still on the physical boundary of our body, the envelope of our skin.

The second aspect of Somatic Meditation is exploring—with openness and acceptance, and without any prejudice, judgment, or conscious agenda whatsoever—what we discover when we are paying attention to our body in this manner. This is no simple thing, especially since our entire conscious life as humans is typically maintained and protected by the "ego thing"—by *not* paying attention in this open and unrestricted way. Rather, we habitually direct our attention away from our body and its raw, infinitely expanding, unprocessed experience to our thinking mind with its labeling, judging, contextualizing, and narrativizing of more or less everything our body knows, thus severely limiting and hiding from our conscious awareness what is actually, somatically there.

So step one in Somatic Meditation is to come to and into the body and attend; and then step two is to open our consciousness into the interior wakefulness that is going on under the surface. Perhaps the notion of the inherent wakefulness of the body—its enlightenment or essentially realized state—may strike the reader as unfamiliar, slightly mystifying, or even implausible. I hope that by the end of this book you will have a much more clear and concrete understanding and, more importantly, experiential sense of what I am talking about.

These two aspects of Somatic Meditation I have just described correspond to what are traditionally called "mindfulness" (*shamatha*) and "awareness" (*vipashyana*), found in virtually all forms of Buddhist meditation. In most conventional teaching of mindfulness, the body is generally left out, despite some body-focused elements such as attending to the breath or the occasional use of body scans—as in the work of the popular *vipashyana* meditation teacher S. N. Goenka (1924–2013). While such approaches are helpful up to a point, they are limited because for them the body is typically a stepping stone to something else, rather than being an object of exploration in and of itself. When examined on its own terms, we discover that the body has many internal dimensions that are hidden to the superficial view and many layers or levels of experience beneath the obvious sensations.

The situation in relation to meditation and the body is quite confusing because, given the increasing importance attributed to "the body" in contemporary culture these days, nearly every meditation teacher wants to say they are including the body—but such claims raise some important questions. The body is included to what extent and in what ways? Does the instruction really move us definitively away from the left-brain orientation? And has anything fundamentally changed in the practitioner's process and maturation? Meditation that is truly somatic always implies radical change and transformation in our state of being.

The unfortunate result of underplaying the body in its totality in much mindfulness and awareness instruction is that we are not really addressing, let alone working through, the pernicious and debilitating disembodiment that afflicts virtually everyone in modern societies, a disembodiment that sabotages our physical, emotional, social, and spiritual well-being. When the meditator does not address his or her disembodiment in a fundamental and decisive way, particularly on the spiritual level, any kind of meditation carried out is more than likely to lead eventually to the complete cul-de-sac of disconnection and disassociation—a dead end from which, because of sophisticated techniques and defensive rationalizations that can be built up in the practice itself, escape is extremely difficult.

When we approach meditation as an essentially—I would almost say "purely"—somatic discipline, then everything changes. Most important, the spiritual journey is now seen not as separating oneself from "samsara," from all that is physical, worldly, impure, and problematic, but (quite to the contrary) as a process of deeper and deeper entry into those very domains of our existence. When we do, we discover that it is precisely within the interior reality of those aspects of our fully embodied, visceral life that our most important discoveries occur, our true spiritual journey can unfold, and lasting, all-inclusive transformation is able to come about.

In fact, authentic realization, we see, can *only* happen when we abandon the outside standpoint of our left-brain, judging, ego mind and plunge into the innermost depths of our ordinary, unprocessed human experience. As the realized Indian tantric master Tilopa said to his uptight, ever "correct," scholarly disciple Naropa a long time ago, "Naropa, your problem is not *what* you experience; it's that you are taking the *wrong approach* to what you experience. You don't know how to leave it alone." Naropa, the paragon of all of us left-brain junkies, was trying to get rid of his pain by thinking his way out. He was trying to impose now this conceptual map, now that, in an attempt to interpret, limit, and control his experience. He was striving for a fanciful nirvana where he wouldn't have to deal with the messiness of his own life any more. And so he was running away from the very place where, alone, genuine realization can occur.

Everything that I teach, the entire journey involved in the somatic work, is essentially a meditation practicum; it is a series of

Somatic Meditation exercises and practices designed to lead you into the magnificent and stunning spiritual journey that is your own, and yours alone, to discover and to make, waiting for you within your body. Some of these somatic protocols, as I call them, may correspond to what you think of as meditation, and many may not. As an example of the latter, in many of the practices described below, you will be asked to lie down and direct your mind to all kinds of unexpected and even quite unknown parts of your body; you may not think of this as meditation practice, but it is. Similarly, in this book you will find practices you can do in bed—going to sleep, waking up in the middle of the night, or in the midst of insomnia—and practices you can look to in the midst of heated interpersonal interaction or even intense, traumatic recall. And they are all about the body. In other aspects of my teaching, once a solid foundation of somatic presence and awareness has been established, we are able to work most fruitfully with more commonly recognizable meditation practices, such as sitting on a cushion in traditional meditation postures. Without somatic training and awareness, though, the outcomes of more conventional practice will be limited; but with such training and awareness, there is no limit to the meditative journey you can make.

However familiar or unfamiliar such practices may seem, however much they do or do not fit in with what you may be thinking of as meditation, they are all equally "meditation": they are all dimensions of the practice of somatic mindfulness and somatic awareness mentioned above. You can practice mindfulness and awareness in any position and in any situation, and everything can become a domain of your own maturation and awakening. This is the message of the somatic lineage.

In this book, I am going to teach you the foundation of the various forms of Somatic Meditation that we practice in our lineage. This foundation is a corpus of fundamental somatic protocols—body-based meditation practices—that show us how to come with attention to the body (mindfulness) and then surrender into that somatic arena, opening ourselves to what the body wants to show us, what it wants us to know (awareness). What I aim for us to discover in the following chapters is that our body as a whole, as well as any part of it, is not an objectifiable, quantifiable reality, but rather a "gate," a portal and a process through which much larger domains of our being, and of Being itself, become accessible to us. In the view of the somatic lineage, the body is not only the temple of enlightenment but also the one and only gateway to knowing, touching, surrendering into, and identifying with the Totality of Being. This is what enlightenment truly means. As we say in our lineage, inspired by the most advanced teachings of Tibetan Buddhism (Dzogchen), "true spiritual realization, authentic enlightenment, is found in the body and nowhere else."[1]

The array of somatic protocols described in this book is not just a *foundation* for the journey of somatic awakening that I teach. Far more than this, it actually *includes within itself* the entire journey to full realization—and I have a hunch that, in the course of this book, you may well be able to experience much of this for yourself. All the other somatic practices we do in our lineage are further clarifications of what is already fully present in what I am about to teach you; they are enhancements of the fundamental training that is offered here. This book will enable you to enter into the limitless world of the Soma. Once you have done that, experientially of course, then I will feel that my job is done. You will be "dialed in," as they say, to the endless possibilities of your incarnation, and you will have important tools wherever you go and whatever you do toward your further awakening.

2

To Be a Body

My principal meditation teacher was Chögyam Trungpa Rinpoche, one of the first Tibetan lamas to present meditation in the West. During the seventeen years that I knew him, from 1970 until his death in 1987, he transmitted the somatic Vajrayana lineage to me and his other senior students. Since his death, I have been fortunate to have the time and the opportunity to explore extensively Rinpoche's transmission through study, practice, and most importantly, teaching, where I have learned the most.

One single concept best characterizes the instruction that Rinpoche received from his teachers and that he wanted to pass on to his students: "embodied spirituality." But in using this term, what are we talking about? The somatic approach teaches that the spiritual is already, from the beginning, implicit within what we call the material—not only in our own physical body but also (as we shall discuss further below) in the larger body of our incarnate situation in the cosmos. This means that the essential nature of our incarnational materiality, both what is inside (body) and what is outside (cosmos), is already primordially and inherently spiritual. Trungpa Rinpoche taught that authentic spirituality cannot exist apart from embodied reality because disembodied spirituality is exclusive, separationist, and incomplete. Any attempt to present spirituality as disembodied is a bogus spirituality, a conceptualized, self-serving construct; at the end of the day, it is simply ego's game, all over again, just on a subtler and more hidden level, what Trungpa called "spiritual materialism."

The somatic view of Vajrayana Buddhism has revolutionary implications for our meditation practice as modern people and for our spiritual journey altogether. As mentioned, it means that our spiritual life, far from involving a distancing and separating from our body and all the realities of our physical incarnation, requires just the opposite: we must turn toward our body and our life as the proper and only possible arena for authentic spiritual development—as the only place where our path can unfold and as the only possible true access point for our genuine realization. Anything else is a chimera, a dream. When I talk about embodied spirituality in this book, then, I mean that connecting with our body and our ordinary life are not add-ons: they *are* the practice of spirituality; they are what the spiritual journey is all about.

The somatic point of view is that the spiritual journey can only really begin within the depths of our incarnation; that we make the full journey only by exploring our own actual experience as an incarnational being, as it progressively discloses itself in our practice and our life; and that, in the end, this body is what we realize in all of its dimensions, in all of its subtlety and depth. This is the ultimate spiritual illumination, the long-sought elixir of life, the realization of nirvana. There isn't anything beyond this for, as I hope to show you, this is the illumination of the Totality of Being.

We can further clarify what embodied spirituality is by seeing what it isn't. In many of the traditional religions of both West and East, including many forms of Buddhism, the spiritual life is understood as a process of separating oneself from everything that is problematic and nonspiritual in order to gain higher, "spiritual" states of meditative awareness. And what are these nonspiritual things that one is separating oneself from? All that seems ordinary, mundane, and "worldly"; the body and all that is seated in it, including instincts and sensations; feelings, emotions, and bodily perceptions; human attachment and sexuality; all that feels potentially problematic, chaotic, and obstructive in our life, all that triggers us, activates us, and stirs us up and leaves us feeling confused, troubled, and incomplete.

Meditation is often viewed as a way to separate ourselves from all of this and rise above it, to get to an altitude where we can relax into a space that is unobstructed and peaceful. This goal of separation seems to reflect a somewhat negative attitude toward our regular life and the ordinary world as if, at least in a spiritual sense, those things don't hold very much of importance for us. And so we often practice meditation as a process of progressive distancing and disembodiment, where we are employing meditative techniques to separate what we feel are the "higher" part of ourselves—our more pure, clear, and clean parts—from everything that is lower—all the mundane, ordinary, pained, nagging, struggling parts. This approach leads, as mentioned, to a state of spiritual dissociation.

The process might look like this. We sit down to meditate and use a technique to try to calm the distress and chaos in our mind, disturbances perhaps fueled by our compulsive thinking, painful memories of unresolved situations or relationships, aggressive competitiveness, and distressing feelings and emotions. We try to smooth the turbulence of all the things that seem to be closing in on us, suffocating us, creating an intense claustrophobia. This tranquilization of our minds is a well-known practice in Buddhism called *shamatha,* or mindfulness, mentioned earlier. The powerful techniques for this can indeed induce the desired effects and, as our minds begin to quiet down, we may then enjoy a more peaceful and open state.

But here is where things get very tricky: the practice of meditation as a process of tranquilization typically implies a conscious intention, a mental image of what we are looking for, and
a process of deliberate inclusion and exclusion leading us toward
our desired spiritual goal. This is tricky because of our remarkable
human capacity to limit and control experience: witness the
human ego itself. It has been estimated that out of every million
parts of information received and processed by our body, we
humans only admit thirteen parts into our conscious awareness.
That means we only allow ourselves to be conscious of .000013
percent of the data, of experience, known to our body. That capacity to limit and control our experience is operational in the
way mindfulness is practiced by many of us, although we may be
quite unconscious of this fact. What often happens with many of
us is that we are able, with sufficient discipline and willpower, to
get ourselves into something like the desired state; but it takes a
tremendous amount of effort of separation and exclusion of everything else to get there and it leaves us in a bit of a trance.

The positive benefits of this kind of meditation should not be
minimized; to have a way to separate ourselves, at least for a time,
from all that is problematic and painful in ourselves and our lives,
to have a safe haven to retreat to in the midst of life's storms, to be
able to rest and recuperate, can have considerable benefits. This
kind of meditation thus becomes a powerful panacea helping us
to remove ourselves from the more seamy and squalid, the more
difficult and anxiety-ridden realities of daily life: "What a relief!"
Some would argue—some do argue—that this is exactly what
meditation is for and, for that reason, we should enthusiastically
embrace the capacity it gives us to step out and temporarily
dissociate, to disembody, from our embedded, bodily existence.
Meditation in this sense is clearly an oasis and an important one
in our life, but, as Nietzsche famously remarked, "Where there are
oases, there are also idols."

Taking us in quite another direction, the somatic teachings see the spiritual life as a journey toward ever fuller and more complete intimacy and even identification with our human incarnation—and we are not talking about just the "nice" parts. This means surrendering our separate spiritual stance, our "spiritual" self, and falling into contact, communication, alignment, and, finally, union with the most ordinary, basic aspects of our human existence, as they are. These include everything we go through, our whole somatic existence, with its sensations, bodily perceptions, feelings, and emotions—including all of our ordinary mental life, the ups and downs, the confusion, the pleasure and pain, everything.

For somatic spirituality, our problem is not, as in conventional spirituality, that we are too close to these mundane features of our life but rather that we are too far away from them; our problem is not that we are too embodied (the disembodied approach), but that we are not embodied enough. The only place we can truly, authentically, and fully wake up is in the midst of life—right in the middle of our quotidian life, exactly as it is. The somatic lineage is thus life-affirming to an absolute degree; it is, in Trungpa Rinpoche's words, "ultimate positivity": we walk the path toward realization by abandoning any sense of distinction between our spiritual journey and our life journey that consists of the specific, gritty realities of our ordinary existence; in fact they are one and the same.

Many writers in our contemporary culture are articulating these or similar ideas. However, simply having this perspective on a purely intellectual or conceptual level is going to be of limited help for ourselves or our world. If, on the contrary, through the somatic methods, we come to see and experience this for ourselves, it changes everything. We no longer need to be minimizing or denying large parts of ourselves or be engaged in a constant struggle to free ourselves from the mundane aspects of ourselves and our lives. Quite the opposite, we are now fully and thoroughly liberated into a complete acceptance and openness to everything we are, to see for ourselves that everything we go through is an engagement with the heart of reality itself. Moreover, the somatic approach shows us how to meet the most painful and problematic situations, emotions, and people in our life and to find within those difficult aspects of our life the next step on our path or spiritual journey. In short, to see the grittiness of the world and, more than that, to experience it directly as the blessing we have been searching for.

The approach of somatic spirituality shows us how to transform the yuck and poison of our own negativity into something fresh, wholesome, and creative. And then, finally, the most simple and ordinary aspects of our human experience become sources of insight, freedom and joy, and revelations of the deepest mysteries of the universe. Thus it is that if we turn our back on our body and our bodily existence—on the ordinary, the commonplace, and mundane—we are turning our back on what is ultimately and finally real; we are giving up our one opportunity to find our own true and destined place within the infinity of being.

3

Consider Your Body's Mind

Until quite recently it has been the assumption in Western cultures that mind and body are two distinct and separate realities. This belief is, of course, inseparable from the presumption that spirituality is based in the mind and involves separating and distancing oneself from the body and all things earthly. Largely through the discoveries of neuroscience and neuropsychology, a consensus has emerged that this dualistic way of looking at mind and body is invalid. We now know that the body itself is intelligent and aware, down to the cellular level. So there is no body that is in some sense not equally and at the same time "mind." And the mind, rather than being a separate entity, is intimately connected with, if not reducible to, the collective awareness of the neurological network of the body; so there is no mind that is not, at the same time, the body.

The scientific conversation about "body" and "mind" has been evolving in some very interesting directions. For example, consider the terms "left brain" and "right brain." Since the mid-nineteenth century anatomists have recognized that the two hemispheres of our brain operate quite differently and know things in two very distinct but complementary ways. These two hemispheres have been termed "the left brain" and "the right brain."

Our left brain is typically described as housing "our conscious self"[1] or our "ego mind"[2]; it is often said to be characterized by "the three L's"; it is linear, logical, and linguistic. It is the seat of discursive thought. As such, it is a more or less disembodied, autonomous, closed system, cycling and recycling already existing information that exists in its database in the form of memories, ideations, labeling, judgments, and conceptual abstractions of all sorts. It houses the function of language, both spoken and written. As the seat of our ego consciousness it carries out executive, managerial, and coping functions. Not surprisingly, the left brain is neurologically the most far removed from our body and its direct perceptual experience, a fact that can be seen both experientially and anatomically. The left brain is not an originator or a source; it is a processor: it cannot feel, sense, or experience anything directly; and it is connected to the right brain only by a few neurological pathways.

Our right brain, by contrast, is our "physical, emotional self."[3] It is deeply grounded in our body and is all about direct, unmediated, nonconceptual experience. It beholds things within a field of infinite silence and space, without any judgment or evaluation, without any discursive processing whatsoever. It receives experience of this moment in its totality, without any boundaries or filtering.[4] It is like a mirror that simply reflects. The neuroscientist and stroke survivor Jill Bolte Taylor explains that the right brain "takes things as they are and acknowledges what is in the present."[5] Everything is there as in a collage and the interconnections of everything are seen.[6] Lacking conceptual reference points, the right brain has no sense of past, present, or future: this moment is experienced as timeless.[7]

Neuroscientists are also using some other roughly equivalent but more nuanced terms to refer to the same thing. They are doing so because, while the two modalities of knowing described above are relatively clear, locating them exclusively in the right and left hemispheres is problematic. In fact, these two ways of knowing, while primarily associated with the two hemispheres, actually involve a much more geographically diverse spread throughout the entire brain and beyond that, for the "right brain," the entire neurological network of our body—to the point that even talking about a right "brain" may be questionable.

Thus some neuroscientists are now talking about two "functions," rather than two hemispheric locales, of the two ways of knowing. One is the function of the conceptualizing, abstracting, executive, conscious ego mind, which is primarily associated with the left hemisphere, and the other is the function of the holistic, nonconceptual awareness of the body, which is more closely associated with the right hemisphere but includes our entire subcortical neurological system.

Following this functional way of looking at the brain, neuroscientists are also speaking of "top down" versus "bottom up" knowing. "Bottom up" functioning refers to the way in which direct, unmediated experience arises out of the unconscious domain of the body ("right brain"). "Top down" refers to the conscious, ego mind's function of conceptual processing of what arises from the body, whereby we select from our inventory of labels, abstractions, judgments, and preconceptions those most fitting to "knowing conceptually" and mapping a selection of the nonconceptual experience that is arriving at the boundary of consciousness ("left brain").

Other neuroscientists are using terms (very interesting in the present context) that suggest the *experience* of these two levels or modes of knowing (rather than geography or function). I want to draw attention to that approach here, because this distinction in the experiential quality is especially important for understanding the somatic journey. In particular, the terms they use for these ways of knowing are "exogenous" and "endogenous." "Exogenous" means "arriving from the outside," and it points to "right brain" or bottom-up knowing, an experience of utter unfamiliarity: we feel as if information is arriving from outside of the domain of our familiar, conscious, ego world, coming as new and as yet unprocessed, undomesticated (by our ego). Exogenous refers to phenomena that arise naturally and spontaneously from the darkness and the unknown (i.e., subcortical and largely unconscious) regions of our body: feelings, sensations, intuitions, "felt-senses," visceral impressions, somatic memories—arriving in our awareness in a direct, fresh, immediate, and naked way. Neuroscientists speak of "exogenous stimulae."

By contrast, "endogenous" means "coming from the inside," which refers to coming from within the already existing and known database of the "left brain," the self-conscious, self-referential ego. Endogenous thus points to what we recognize as familiar—experience mediated by and filtered through ideas, concepts, assumptions, judgments, conclusions that already exist in our consciousness, based on the past, through which we process our present experience in order to "know," manage, and control it. Endogenous involves top-down application of the familiar so that we can label, conceptualize, and pin down the unfamiliar and— to ego—potentially threatening and destabilizing influx of the unknown. Neuroscientists refer to "endogenous control." An understanding of these two very different modalities of knowing are at the core of the somatic approach and, throughout this book, I want you to keep these neuroscientific concepts in the back of your mind to help your understanding of the journey we will be making.

In the following pages, I will be discussing these two modes of knowing but, following a more somatic, experiential way of speaking, will distinguish them as the "left brain," on the one hand, and as the "Soma," or body (rather than the "right brain"), on the other. I prefer these terms because, while the functions of the conscious, ego mind are indeed primarily located in the left hemisphere, the functions typically associated with the "right brain," as already suggested, are in fact distributed throughout the entire body: though largely unconscious in most of us, they occur through a vast network of somatically known and knowing experience and processing, of a system of awareness that includes aspects of the right cerebral hemisphere, the limbic system, the brain stem, the heart, the gut, the organs, the bones, the fascia, and, as mentioned, extending down to each cell in our body.

The discoveries of neuroscience, then, provide an important bridge for us to understand how the body is viewed in this lineage. Both neuroscience and somatic spirituality agree that the body (including the right brain) is the realm of direct experience. For both, the body receives and registers experience before we think about it, before we process it. The body thus knows experience in a pure and unmediated way. It sees things as they are, as if in a mirror, independent of the causal networks of past, present, and future. The body's way of knowing is holistic; through an extensive openness and a nearly infinite sensitivity, it reflects the Totality of what is and it knows the interconnection of everything.

But a critical distinction exists between the approach of neuroscience and the approach of Somatic Meditation. Neuroscience is based on what can be observed and proved in controlled experiments and therefore looks at the body from the outside. The approach of Somatic Meditation, by contrast, looks at the body from the inside, a process called "interoception" in neuropsychology. Science comes to its conclusions based on observation of the body as an external object, defined by identifiable causes and conditions; Somatic Meditation makes its journey by observing the body from the inside as a kind of ultimate, all-knowing subject and a limitless source of knowledge in the form of direct perception.

At the same time, the distinction is about the differences in the two approaches, not about the people who may employ them. For example, increasing numbers of modern therapists, scientists, and philosophers are not only fully cognizant of the interior, interoceptive perspective but are guided in their professional work at least partly by what they themselves have observed, in their direct experience of their own bodies.

To cite just one example, the philosopher and psychologist Eugene Gendlin, the creator of a therapeutic approach called "Focusing," beautifully clarifies the nature and character of what is known through interoception, the viewing and experiencing of the body from the inside. Gendlin has developed the widely influential notion of "felt sense," referring to what the body knows directly of itself, without the mediation of the thinking mind. For Gendlin, the felt sense, the ability to know one's own interior, somatic experience, is the open sesame of successful psychotherapies.

Through the methods of Somatic Meditation, we learn how to extend our awareness into our body and we begin to sense what is there—although "extending our awareness into" doesn't quite catch it. In fact, through the Soma-based practices we are softening the boundary between our highly intentional, restricted, conscious ego mind and the limitless, unconscious domain of the body. When we do this, our conscious mind begins to tap into and connect with the somatic awareness that is already going on—mostly unbeknownst to us—in our body. In this larger field of consciousness, we are still conscious but in a very different way.

It is as if we are waking up, within our Soma, and we suddenly find ourselves in a new world. We are uncovering a completely different experience of what our body is. We begin to see that what we formerly took to be our body was just a made-up version with little correspondence to anything real. We find in our body previously unimaginable vistas of spaciousness, experience arising that is ever surprising and fresh, an endless world of possibilities for ourselves and our lives.

In the practice of Somatic Meditation, simply in learning how to come into our body and inhabit it with awareness, we are already entering the embodied spiritual journey. Being within our Soma in this way enables us to meet our experience directly, to receive the pure experience of our life, and this, right away and without our doing anything else, plunges us into a process of spiritual discovery that is inspiring, compelling, and deeply fulfilling.

When I use the term "Soma," then, I intend to refer, interoceptively, to the field of experience that opens up when we descend beneath the surface of conceptual thinking into the still depths of our body. The body we will be exploring together, the Soma, is what is experienced when we set aside all our thinking about the body and let ourselves drop into its own awareness, its own way of knowing. This is a kind of knowing that does not rely upon and is, in fact, completely independent of conceptual thinking. Just what that is and how we can receive it, and what it can mean for us is, in short, the journey of this book.

When we explore our body—the Soma—from the inside, we enter into a seemingly endless series of discoveries about what it means for us to have a body, to be a body. For example, we find in the body an objective witness to our life that has no investment whatsoever in our skewed ego-versions of things. In addition, our Soma not only knows the truth of how it is with us, others, and the world, but it appreciates and, in a strange way, delights in everything. Even more, it wants to communicate this to us and provide mentoring. Our Soma is literally an infinite ocean of practical wisdom, and it offers itself as a guide for our life that is impartial, resourceful, and utterly reliable. I hope all of this will become clear through the somatic journey described in this book.

Through the somatic work covered here, it should eventually dawn on us—perhaps gradually, perhaps suddenly—that our Soma is actually not bounded by the envelope of our skin or by anything else. In other words, when we have direct experiential contact with our body, we actually discover that our Soma has no definitive boundaries at all. We think it has boundaries simply because that idea is based on our conditioning; but in fact, it turns out, when we actually take a look, it is our thoughts alone that unnecessarily limit and freeze our experience of our body into such a small compass. Through the somatic journey, we discover that our body is not only open to the universe beyond; in fact, we gradually come to see—to *experience*, actually—that the only meaningful way to describe our body at that point is that the body of the universe and our body are inseparable, dimensions of one and the same reality. This "infinity of the body" is not a theory; it is an experiential datum, and when you realize this state of affairs about your body, as did the neuroscientist Jill Bolte Taylor, it completely changes your experience and understanding of being human as it did hers.

In a body-based spirituality, then, when we approach the Soma from the inside, without any conceptual overlay or interference, we come face-to-face with the body's inherent, primordial wakefulness. For somatic spirituality, the Soma is the realm of enlightenment, of ultimate realization.

The somatic protocols described below show us how to make this journey into our body and to discover these ultimate truths and these liberating realities for ourselves, in our own direct experience. In our body, we come upon the resplendent "buddha field" so many have sought throughout the ages. We meet a realm that, far from being "empty," is filled and charged with the grandeur of our own unmediated, naked experience of life in all its variety, its own fullness and mystery. We discover that our own life, from the beginning, has been the free and joyful expression of the universe itself. Within the vast territories of the Soma, then, we are able to witness the final beatitude, the sacredness of all being. This is the fabled nirvana that Buddhist texts have touted for two and a half millennia; we may be surprised to discover, though, that this nirvana is not anything far off or unattainable, but rather it is fully and completely revealed and available, right here and right now, in this very body of ours.

PART TWO

The Six Core Somatic Practices

4

An Overview of the Somatic Protocols

A t this point, I would like to introduce you to some of the most important somatic practices, which I will be referring to as "the body work" or "somatic protocols." In their complete form as practiced in our lineage, they include roughly twenty-five distinct practices each of which can be applied in different ways and at several different levels. In this book, you will be introduced to the six most basic and important of these. The six offered here will provide you with the foundational practices of the entire somatic journey of this lineage, of which all the other protocols are further elaborations and refinements. With these six in hand, you will be able to develop a strong somatic presence and tap into the endless spiritual journey that is waiting for you in your body. These practices enable us to connect with our Soma in a new way; after we have trained, we will find our relationship to our physical body and its subtler dimensions—and our experience of it—in a very different place from where we began.

I have developed this corpus of somatic protocols gradually over the past three and a half decades, drawing upon my own study, practice, and experience as well as the reports of my fellow teachers and students. The basic orientation of the somatic work, as mentioned, derives from Tibetan Vajrayana Buddhism, which is fundamentally somatic in its approach. It is the Tibetan tantra, then, that forms the core inspiration and organizing framework for what follows.

Beyond that, I follow the Tibetan nonsectarian approach to spirituality known as *ri-me,* by incorporating additional methods and techniques in so far as they are able to bring us more deeply into our body and, as the Tibetan tradition says, "relieve suffering and lead to freedom." Hence while I draw principally on Tibetan Vajrayana, other important streams flow into the somatic work. For example, I have had the great good fortune to meet and study with many wonderful meditation teachers—in person and in their recorded and written works—from Vajrayana, Chan, Zen, and Theravada Buddhism. Beyond that, I have learned a great deal about the possibilities of sacred embodiment from several indigenous traditions, including those from North and South America, Africa, and, lately, Hawai'i. Through these studies, I have been able to deepen my understanding of what I received from Trungpa Rinpoche and also to see further into the possibilities of somatic spirituality for our contemporary world.

An additional source of the somatic protocols is spiritual Taoism, which is, perhaps uniquely, a religion of the body (a phrase used by Kristofer Schipper, one of the world's leading Sinologists, in his book, *The Taoist Body*). My incorporation of Taoist techniques and perspectives has been made possible by my Taoist teachers, but it also comes from my own study, practice, and exploration of Taoism as recorded in the literary tradition. Finally, the somatic protocols have been nourished by the increasingly rich and creative modern Western traditions of somatic exploration and healing—for me this includes principally Hakomi but also other similar somatic therapies such as Feldenkrais, Rolfing, Alexander work, Continuum

Movement, Integrative Manual Therapy, Focusing, and other forms of body-based awareness training that I have studied over the years.

It has taken me most of my adult life to learn, explore, and understand what these various somatic traditions are about and what each shows us about the body and the spiritual journey. Over time, through my own practice and through teaching many thousands of people directly, I have come to see how, when properly positioned as the foundational stage of the spiritual quest, these various streams of somatic spirituality can come together to provide a coherent, integrated, and powerful vehicle for thoroughly grounding ourselves in our body and beginning to explore the spiritual possibilities of the Soma. By this time, the corpus of protocols is sufficiently mature, functional, and serviceable—and proven—so that I can have confidence in offering it to you here.

The somatic training outlined here is entirely nonsectarian. Although I have derived the main inspiration, orientation, and practices from Tibetan tradition, this is not Tibetan Buddhism. In spite of the fact that I have drawn on other Buddhist practice-oriented lineages, the training here is not any of those forms of Buddhism, either. While other religious traditions have been important resources for me, what you will find here is not religious. The formal religious traditions of the past and present have, too often, proposed to own our minds, but—in spite of occasional claims to the contrary—none of them can own our bodies. The naked, nonconceptual experience of our own actual life is ours and ours alone, and when we realize that, we are freed from all the prisons of past templates, conventional thinking, and religious dogmatism. We are set free to fly.

We may, indeed we must—with all honor and due respect—take our inspiration and our lead from the teachings, the practices, the records—and the creativity—of the past. But what we are called to here is not to imitate the past or try to live within it in any way; we are called to something new. The task before us is, in short, to find our way down, through the mire and obfuscation of everything we have thought and think, into the fertile and ever-unknown underground of our raw human experience. The task seems daunting; but the training to do just that is offered right here.

How to Work with the Practices and the Guided Audio Recordings

This part of the book provides the written instructions, along with important explanations and clarifications, for the six basic somatic practices. But for you, the reader, this is just the beginning, for these instructions only lay the groundwork for a full, somatic understanding of the protocols. In order to help you take the next step, we are providing audio guided meditations for each of these six protocols on the Shambhala Publications website at www.shambhala.com/theawakeningbody. In order to fully assimilate what this book offers, it will be essential that you listen to the guided meditations and follow their practice instructions as you do so. (In addition, you can explore these and the other somatic protocols in other free and for-purchase guided meditations on the Dharma Ocean website (www.dharmaocean.org), through online Dharma Ocean courses, and through in-person programs at Dharma Ocean's Blazing Mountain retreat center in Crestone, Colorado, and elsewhere in Dharma Ocean programs in North America and beyond.)

The written instructions and the oral instructions offer complementary but also quite distinct means of access to the practices. The written instructions provide a conceptual map of the territory to be explored. As maps, they are most important because they give us the basic coordinates and steps of each practice. *But, to say it again, the map is not the territory.* The oral, guided meditations uniquely provide a way for you to actually enter directly into the territory of the body itself, so that we can know, experientially, what these practices are really about, how they feel, and what they accomplish.

To use a traditional Tibetan example, in the oral, guided meditations what is being offered is what is known as "direct transmission." Transmission in this case means the teacher, as catalyst, making available to the student the full, naked experience of the teachings. Until we experience, for ourselves and in our body, what is being taught, we don't really understand it, we aren't assimilating it and, most importantly, we don't fundamentally change. The ultimate transformation we are looking for eludes us.

In looking just at the map, we employ our visual faculty, our sight to read and our conceptual, conscious mind to "see." Often we take this kind of experience, of seeing what is being said, to be the basic reality of it, but it isn't. Though we may not realize it, we are still just dealing with the map. But the minute the human voice comes into play, everything changes.

The human voice holds within it the entire experiential reality of the speaker. That is to say, when we speak to another person, though we generally do not realize it, we are transmitting the totality of our experience. And though the hearer may not be conscious of it, his or her body is taking in the totality of the speaker's experience. Sometimes, however, we are conscious of it: have you ever had an experience in which someone has been describing an incident, an encounter, a situation, and, with only a few words out of the speaker's mouth, you have seen within yourself, you have experienced directly, what is being talked about?

In listening to and following the audio guided meditations, then, you are entering the world of transmission. You will be receiving, partly consciously and partly unconsciously, the experience, the actual territory, of each practice. The totality of my own experience and realization of this lineage, received from Trungpa

Rinpoche as I listened to him, and by him from his teachers, will be coming through to you. It is significant that this "listening" or "hearing" transmission began with the Buddha himself and his experience, and it is said to have come down through the generations to us.

There are some additional reasons that the guided audio meditations will be helpful. For one thing, the audio versions are easier to follow because you will be able to concentrate on the instructions as they are being given rather than having to refer back to a printed page at each step. In addition, the audio versions contain only the practice instructions. By contrast, the written versions below contain additional explanation and this could be distracting to the practices. Beyond that, in the audio versions, I am able to sequence the instructions so you have an appropriate amount of time to explore each part before being asked to move on. And finally, in the audio version, I can provide additional instructions that are not possible here.

I suggest reading through what I have written by way of commentary in the introductions to each practice and also the written practice instructions. Then, try the practice for yourself, ideally listening to the guided audio meditation.

The six somatic protocols that I am about to teach you are generally to be practiced in a sequential way because, in a progressive and unfolding manner, they address different areas of our disembodiment. Ten Points (practice 1), for example, addresses our general lack of awareness of our overall body. The practice works with the body as a whole, sometimes strictly through attention, sometimes also including breath. A second practice, that of Earth Descent (practice 2), uses both attention and breath, seeking to establish an energetic connection with the earth and a direct experience of the synergistic relation of earth and body; this helps create a deeper sense of groundedness, well-being, and autonomic confidence than we can achieve if we are conscious only of our physical body and hold our awareness strictly within the envelope of our skin. Importantly, the more connected we feel to the earth, the more stabilized, secure, and protected we feel and the more fully and easily we are able to extend our awareness into and consciously inhabit our body, our experience, and our life.

A further group of practices explores the interior of the body, including the sensations, the energy, and the experiences of interior space. To open up the interior vistas, I will teach you Yin Breathing (practice 3), Central Channel (practice 4), and Whole Body Breathing and Rooting (practice 5). Beyond this, Twelvefold Lower-Belly Breathing (practice 6) will help enhance our experience of the inner space of our body.

Learning and practicing the six foundational protocols will enable you to bring the Somatic Meditation approach into any other contemplative or meditative practice you may be engaged in. When you do, you will notice that whatever you are doing becomes much more intensely experiential, grounded, and *real,* with far more transformational power. For instance, if you have been feeling that your meditation, prayer, or contemplation practice just isn't very satisfying, you may discover that it is not your tradition that was the problem but the way you were practicing it. Sometimes we are way too much up in our heads. It is quite amazing how this somatic work can, in a very simple way, bring new dimensions of life to whatever you are doing.

To bring all of this back to the language of neuroscience, experience may be described as the occurrence of certain neurons firing in particular patterns. Because we are directing our attention and connecting with our body in new ways through these protocols, it means neural growth is occurring and our neurological system is developing new capacities. Neural growth involves not only the production of new neurons but also the enhancement of existing neural pathways or new development of neural pathways and networks of interaction and information processing. All of this changes the structure of our psychophysiological system in ways that can be measured, as well as its ability to experience, know, and function in new ways.

Through the somatic protocols and the neurological development they lead to, new information is going to arrive to our consciousness; we are extending our awareness further and further into the previously uncharted, unconscious darkness of our body. But, importantly, it not just that we are gaining access to the huge amount of information currently residing in our body in the darkness of our unconscious. Far more than that, through developing new neurons and new neurological pathways, we are developing new capabilities to receive and process and hence to know and to experience, throughout our entire somatic system. These capabilities did not exist before anywhere in our state of being; they really are new. In this, we are truly enhancing our experience of being human. We are developing and maturing our ability to feel and to know our life, developing and maturing our capacity to know, in an unmediated and nonconceptual way—in our Soma— the illimitable universe that we live in, of which we currently may have rather little direct or personal knowledge.

5

Practice One: Ten Points

OVERVIEW

Ten Points is the first somatic protocol that we teach because it is the most basic and also the most complete, containing within it at least implicitly all the other body practices. After you have trained in all six protocols offered here, you will find that when you return to Ten Points, you will be able to practice it and include within it what you have learned in the other five. Thus Ten Points can be practiced at a beginning level but is extraordinarily valuable even if you have been practicing Somatic Meditation for years. To this day, it remains my favorite protocol and, when I teach programs, I almost always begin with it.

Somatic Meditation, no matter what aspect we may be practicing, unfolds in several steps that we will look at more closely below. Briefly, these include the following:

1. Making contact with the body by directing our attention there. Most of the time, it is going to be one part or area we are attending to.

2. Trying to feel what physical sensations are going on there.

3. Beginning to notice tension in that place or area or, if we are working with the body as a whole, as a total body phenomenon.

4. Learning how to place our awareness *within* the tension, experiencing it and inhabiting it from within.

5. Discovering that when we do so, we begin to gain agency over what might have previously seemed to be autonomous tension, outside of our conscious reach.

6. Beginning to soften, dissolve, and release the tension in question.

7. Then noticing what happens when we do, what we discover on the other side of the tension. One thing that tends to occur in Ten Points is that we begin to notice how our bodily sensations *actually* feel, their insubstantial quality; how they are impermanent, fluid, ever changing and even, eventually, intangible and ineffable. Step seven is where the body work proper begins; step seven opens the gate of the body in its largest sense and the somatic journey is our exploration once we step through this gate. In Ten Points, even at the very beginning, we may have glimpses of this larger, indeed infinite, world on the other side.

Ten Points includes, though in a rather concise form, all of these steps and is therefore a most fitting practice as our first one. Shortly, we will be looking at Ten Points in more detail. At this point, though, before turning directly to the practice, I want to offer a little more general explanation.

We're going to direct our attention to various parts of our body, beginning with the feet, and try to feel, to be aware of, what is going on there. The basic principle is that when you put your awareness into a part of your body, something important happens. Though you may feel completely numb at the outset, you begin to develop an increasing ability to feel, in a direct, visceral sense, what is happening in that part of your body. What we are doing, in fact, is consciously tuning in to an awareness that is already present in that part of the body—say, the feet. It is just that, up until now, because we weren't paying attention, we didn't notice. Because we weren't attending the neural pathways connecting our conscious awareness with the somatic awareness of our feet, our sense of our feet went into the "sleep" mode and so we feel numb. But now, by paying attention, those pathways begin to awaken really quite quickly. The more we practice, the more sensitized we become and the more we notice. The process goes on without end and we always have more to discover, even if we are talking about a tiny area of our body.

As we become more and more aware of the parts of our body, at a certain point we will notice something else: the tension in each part. The more we explore this, the more we begin to sense that our entire body is actually riddled with tension. We are talking here not about the natural, healthy tension that is part of being human, but instead we are talking about neurotic tension, elective tension, superimposed tension—superimposed by our conscious orientation, our ego. Neurobiology tells us that that this kind of pathological tension extends all the way down to the cellular level and is a contributing factor to ill health and disease.

So why are we so tense? As we shall see later for ourselves, any naked, unfiltered experience is initially felt to be painful and problematic; without thinking, we try to withdraw from it, evade and get away from it. We do so by literally tensing up, and this tension is everywhere. Why is unfiltered experience painful? Because any new experience is perceived by the conscious ego as a threat. As William Blake observed, human experience in its primal, unprocessed form is infinite. This infinity runs against one of the ego's primary functions, which is to meet the unexpected and, through subverting it into a convenient and safe interpretive framework, to limit and control it and finally, when carried to an extreme, to deny not only its significance but its very existence. When new meditators confess, "I feel so locked up, I don't even know what my life is" or "I feel like I am missing out on the experience of being alive," they speak the truth.

Tensing up is a way of avoiding the unadorned experience and the discomfort it brings ego, whether that discomfort is physical or psychological; tension is our way of closing down experience and shutting off awareness. It is the somatic expression of us holding on to our small ego concept, our restricted, left-brain identity. On the one hand, physically freezing and contracting in tension, and, on the other, psychologically shutting down and hanging on doggedly to our small sense of self are actually the same thing, just manifesting in these two different modes.

In Somatic Meditation we do notice that if we relax physically, our small, ego-centered self begins to soften and relax, becoming less paranoid and rigid; and if we have some familiarity with the meditative process and are able to drop beneath into our larger Self, we relax completely. When we try to meditate in a state of tension, unless the tension is directly, openly, and somatically addressed—and resolved—we are likely to end up feeling that we are skating on the surface. We are still hanging on to ourselves, even coopting our meditation practice in the process; thus, we remain trapped in our little prison, no matter what sophisticated technique we may try.

One of the basic principles of Somatic Meditation, then, is that as we move along the path, our practice involves ever deeper and more complete relaxation. In the Pure Awareness practices of Tibetan Buddhism, it is said that enlightenment can only be attained by relaxing completely. Some who view meditation more in a macho way, as a matter of gritting one's teeth and forcing one's way through obstacles, may feel the approach of utter relaxation to be sloppy and lazy. But I think that is quite a misunderstanding. By relaxing, our awareness opens and we gain access to a fuller and fuller range of our human experience, which means our somatic experience. And that is the goal of meditation and the goal of the spiritual journey itself, at least in the somatic tantric lineages of Tibetan Buddhism. So in Ten Points, we are learning how to connect with our body, discover how we are holding on, and then develop the capacity to release, relax, let go, and see what comes next.

THE PRACTICE

The Basic Lying-Down Position

Begin by taking a lying-down position, on your back, with your knees up and your feet flat on the floor. It is best to lie on a firm surface and the floor is ideal, although some cushioning will likely be needed—having a rug, a blanket, a yoga mat, or some combination of these underneath you will help you be more comfortable. In my teaching, I recommend tying a cord (yoga strap, belt, etc.) around your legs just above the knees so that the knees are just touching; this will allow the psoas muscles to relax and take any strain off your lower back, thus enabling you to relax completely and without any effort at all in the posture.

Now place your hands, palms down, on your lower belly. You can cross your hands one over the other, left hand underneath, right hand on top, or just place them on either side of the lower belly, whichever is more comfortable. Our somatic awareness is rooted in the lower belly and this hand position, owing to the *qi*, *prana*, or knowingness that radiates from the hands, enhances and heightens our general somatic sense. In Ten Points, hands on the lower belly additionally enables the elbows to rest on the earth, which we will need in this practice. Generally, for this and the other protocols carried out in a lying-down position, having eyes closed is best, as that enables you to focus on the internal sensations of your

THE BASIC LYING-DOWN POSTURE.

body enhancing your interoception. However, if you are feeling really drowsy, it can be helpful to open your eyes. You will have to experiment to see what, in each situation, feels best.

This position enables us to work with the "ten points" of our body that are in contact with the earth: the two soles of the feet (points 1 and 2), the two side of the buttocks (3 and 4), the mid-back (5), the two shoulder blades (6 and 7), the two elbows (8 and 9), and the back of the head (10). These are points of energetic contact with the earth, and it doesn't matter if other parts of your body—say your sacrum or mid- to upper back—are also touching the ground under you.

The body work practices are generally first learned and practiced in a lying-down position (the infant position), which I am guiding you in here, and then brought into a sitting-up posture (the adult posture). In the course of this book, here and further on, I will be explaining more about the importance of this distinction and why the training occurs in this order.

Connecting with the Earth under You

Now try to feel the earth under you, solid and supporting, letting your body settle into the feeling. Take a minute or two, just trying to relax into the earth. This position, lying on the back and feeling the earth underneath, is our very early experience as newborns. In this position, we feel the upholding support of the earth under us and are as relaxed, open, and receptive as we will ever be; and, not coincidentally, our neurological development emerging from the practice in this posture will proceed at maximum capacity. Thus, by lying in this position, we are reconnecting with that infant posture but, more than this, we are able to activate the state of being that goes along with it. When we lie in this way, we are notifying the body that it can completely let go, release whatever tension it is carrying, and surrender back into that earliest and most open of all post-birth human states. Reconnecting with this posture and reawakening that somatic sense will be essential throughout all the body work practices that involve lying down.

As we shall presently see, feeling—in a concretely and tangibly somatic way—the support of the earth under us is key to the whole meditative process at whatever stage; the more grounded we feel, the more naturally and effortlessly relaxed and open our body will be, and hence the more open and accepting of our experience we are able to be. By contrast, when we feel disconnected from the earth, the more we feel ungrounded, the more we feel we have to hold ourselves up by sheer ego strength and control our experience. And that breeds the kind of subliminal fear and tension that is counterproductive to meditation. Even when we're lying on the ground, if we're not connecting with the earth, we're still perching, energetically, above the earth; so at this point, please make an effort to open and connect.

Entering Ten Points

In this practice, we are going to use our breath as an aid. We will do this by imagining we are breathing into whatever part of our own body we are working on. We will be visualizing we are breathing into the pores of our skin in that place and bringing the breath—and our awareness—into that place.

So beginning with the feet, put your breath into your big toes, and just try to feel them. Breathing into all the pores of your big toes, feel into your big toe on both feet, and see what you notice. What sensations are there? It doesn't matter how much or how little is there for you; just try to feel more and more into whatever it is. Begin by feeling your socks or, if you have bare feet, what that feels like; feel the temperature, hot, neutral, or cold. Breathing in, try to feel the overall mass of the big toes; then the bottom, the sides, the top of each toe; can you feel the hardness of your toenail? Can you feel into the main body of the big toe? Can you feel the toe bone? Do you feel any discomfort, perhaps an achiness or sharp pains? Take some time to develop this feeling. When we attend to our body in this way, we often uncover all kinds of subtle or not so subtle sensations we never noticed were there.

As you breathe into your big toe, at some point you will notice that you're actually anxiously holding on or gripping, even in your toes! So breathe your awareness into your big toe and begin to feel where you may be holding; where do you feel tension? As you open your awareness into the awareness of the big toe, you will find you can begin to relax the tension that you find in your big toe and let that tension just drain downward into the earth. So the process of release is also the process of relaxation, and through the process of relaxation, through letting the energy into the earth, we connect with the energy of the earth. Strangely enough, releasing in this way connects you with the primordial ground of the earth and deepens that connection.

Now notice any tension in your big toe as a whole. Notice the tension around the joint, and then notice the tension as the big toe enters the foot. Observe that here you have an opportunity to release and relax. As you breathe into your big toe and release, you may find tension in your feet and even up into your thighs releasing because you're creating a flow that will draw tension from the rest of the body down through the big toe and into the earth. As you do this, you may feel called to let your breath slow down. If so, follow the prompt and see how this affects your somatic sense, how present you feel in your body.

Next go through the same process with your second toes. Breathe into the pores of your second toe. Take time to explore the various parts and dimensions of your second toes, just as you did with your big toes. Then see if you can uncover and tap into the tension there. And release. Relax. Let the energy go down . . . into the earth. And then the middle toes. Same process. Breathing in through the pores, feel the middle toe. This toe may be a little more difficult to feel than the big toe or the second toe. Try to breathe your awareness into the middle toe and connect with whatever sensation you find; and in particular, notice the tension in the middle toe and how it actually extends back into the foot. So we're releasing the middle toe. Relaxing.

As you move along, you can always come back to the big toe and the second toe and see if you can release and relax a little bit more. And, as you begin to do this, you'll find, again, elsewhere in the body, opportunities to relax and let go. The body itself wants to release, and the minute we begin to invite that release in our feet, it begins to happen elsewhere. Working with the feet beautifully instigates this process because all the meridians of the body run through the feet. So by working with the feet, you are getting at the whole body.

And now go on to the fourth toe. Again, breathe your awareness in a very deliberate and focused way into the fourth toe. And relax. This toe may feel even more hidden and take a little more effort to sense. And then the baby toe. Take plenty of time with each toe until you find yourself developing a fuller experience of sensations in each toe, its particular tensions, and the process of release. Developing this capacity fully will require many, many iterations, but in each session you should notice an increasing ability to feel and release.

As you release tension in your feet, you are softening the boundary between the darkness of your body and the brightness of your conscious mind, between the limitless unconscious and the bounded conscious mind; in so doing, in a most gentle and natural way, you are also softening the barrier against feelings and experiences you may have been avoiding, denying, or repressing. So it is that you may find various feelings, images, or memories coming up—if so, just welcome them. If they become a little too much, then relax and let the practice go for a while or for today; there is no rush. Assimilate what you need to and then, when you feel ready, return to the practice. In Ten Points practice it is quite rare to run into anything that feels overwhelming, but it can happen. Accessing our larger, as-yet-undiscovered feeling life *through the body* is the safest of all ways to do it, but you do have to go gently and follow the guidance of your body; it will let you know how much is enough and how much is too much. In fact, much trauma therapy is based on this very principle, of helping folks access difficult feeling through the body but in a gentle, step-by-step, gradual manner, moving a little forward into sensation, stepping a little back as needed, giving their conscious awareness plenty of time to become familiar with, assimilate, and integrate unconscious material. Peter Levine, founder of Somatic Experiencing, calls this process "pendulation" and it is a key principle and tool in all the body work I teach.

So now you can just check all five toes and see if there are further opportunities to release. And then we'll come up into the ball of the foot. Again, lots and lots of little points of tension. Begin with the part of the foot right behind the toes. Just where the toes enter the feet, there is going to be a lot of holding and tightness at the junction. See if you can find that. You can go through the junction of each toe and pay attention. Discern the tension, breathe into it, and release. Second toe. Third, fourth, and the baby toe. Then explore farther back into the ball of the foot, looking initially for bare sensation, then looking for tension, and finally letting go. And again, the more you relax the feet, the more you may feel other areas in the body suddenly presenting as tense. There is an invitation here to release those parts and, again, you should follow the somatic prompt. If this occurs, though, don't get sidetracked or diverted; let go and then return to the feet or whatever other part of the body you are working on.

And then we'll come into the arch of the foot. Again, another place where there is a lot of holding. Just feel into its brittleness and rigidity, breathe into it, and release. Then the outside of the foot. Relax. Sometimes in this work, we may forget we need to breathe fully and the breath can become a little shallow. So you can take a deep breath now. Just make sure you're still breathing deeply. Now it may be almost as if there's a river of tension flowing down through the feet and into the earth. Relax, relax, relax. Let go. Then we can go into the very interior of the foot, between the sole of the foot and the instep; notice the density of the interior of the foot, and right in the middle you can find these little crossroads and heavy masses of tension. See if you find those, breathe in, and release them. Just let your whole foot melt. Completely relax your foot and feel it dissolving and melting down into the earth.

Now let's begin to move upward. Include the heel and then the ankles. Let the tension of the heels, then the ankles and anklebones, outside and inside, just flow down through the feet into the earth. Make sure to take plenty of time with each step in the process. When practicing on your own, without my guidance, you might end up spending much of your session on just one area of your body—say your feet and lower legs—to develop your inner somatic sense there further. The gains made by focusing on one area will carry over into your next sessions and other areas. The neurological capacity developed here will stay with you and, in subsequent practice, will be the baseline of somatic awareness in that area from which you start.

And then the shins. Shinbone, muscles on the outside of the shinbone. Breathing into your shinbone, try to put your awareness inside it, for bones hold tension as much or more than our soft tissue. Feel the density. Feel the tension, and let it release. You may be surprised to find you can actually do this and feel the release. Next try to sense the fibula, the smaller bone toward the side of the lower leg. This is really tough to sense, but see if you can. And the muscle on the outside of the shinbone. Feel the tension, breathing in, and let it release down. The calf muscle. Let it release down. Then the knees. So the whole lower leg on both sides is just completely relaxing, surrendering its tension. And, again, you may notice the impact higher up in your body. So check both legs from the soles of your feet up to your knees, and make sure that you are not missing any additional opportunity to release. Scan your foot. Scan your ankles and lower legs and knees. And just let everything go.

So that's it for the first two of Ten Points, the feet. You can see that the feet, because they touch the earth, can act as access points, connecting links to the earth. We are releasing our tension down into the earth but, at the same time, the earth is drawing the tension down into herself. This is because the kind of neurotic tension we are working with is actually the energy of the basic life force that originates up from the earth in the first place and that has gotten trapped in our ego machinery of denial and repression, instead of flowing through. So that energy originates in the earth, flows up through our life process in the form of experience, and seeks to complete itself and return to the source, back down into the earth. But our ego gets in the way and, in its neurotic form, appropriates that life force to try to maintain itself, derailing that energy, and damming it up. That results in what we may call the "pathological ego." (Later we'll talk about the healthy, wholesome ego.)

So this release back into the earth is actually a reflection of the deepest and subtlest dimension of "deep ecology," part of allowing the energy, in the form of our experience, to complete its own life cycle. Our human exploitation of the environment and despoilage of the planet begin right here, misusing the life force in the service of ignorance, aggression, and greed. If we cut the process off right here, in not territorializing and trying to own the life force for ego purposes, we are doing the most ecologically responsible thing we could ever do. Once our exploitation on this basic level is brought to an end, a healthy, effective, and creative ecological consciousness toward the world is the natural and inevitable outcome.

Later, we will discuss how Somatic Meditation provides ways for us to work with, process, and release trauma in an ongoing way; at that point, we will see that the process is the same. By connecting with the earth, as traumatic feelings surface in our consciousness, we are able to liberate them, allow them to complete their journey that was interrupted and put on hold by the traumatic event, and let them flow back into the earth, leaving us unburdened and free.

Now we move on to the next two points, the buttocks on both sides, and then on to the rest of the Ten Points. The process we just went through with the feet and lower legs is the same for the other eight points. I will say a few things about each but, since I have described in so much detail how this practice works with the feet, I am hoping that in your practice you'll be able to apply what we've already learned quite easily to the other eight points.

So now points three and four, the buttocks on both sides. Feel them touching the earth. Breathing into your sitz bones, feel the sensations in as much detail as you can. Notice the tension, then release, relax, let go of the tension. Still using your buttocks as your access points to the earth, come into the perineum. There is generally trauma there for everyone, men and women alike, so go gently and listen to your body. Relax. Release. The anal area. The interior of the lower belly, the region of the genitals, including for men especially the prostate area, and for women especially the cervical area. Next the pubic bone. The whole pelvic cavity, including the hips on the outside. A lot of tension there. Work slowly and carefully with each place; there is so much here for us. Inside of the thighs. Psoas muscle joining the upper inside of the thighs, running through the pelvic cavity to the inside of the lumbar spine. So feel into the pelvic cavity. See where there's tension. See where you're holding on, and release. Let go. You can notice the emotional tone as you do this work. There are many, many discoveries to be made right here, and they all lead in the direction of greater awareness and integration, greater health and well-being. Go slowly and gently, listen to your body—pendulate!— but have confidence in what you find. Your Soma wants to set you free, to live, for your sake and for the sake of Life.

Next the mid-back, point five, will be the connecting place; this will be roughly directly below the solar plexus. The exact location will feel a little different for each of us; see what feels most appropriate for you. Where do you feel most energetically connected with the earth? Breathing in, feel the sensations, then the tension, then let go and release. And then come up to the belly. Let the tension of the front of the belly drift back, melt down through the mid-back into the earth. And we'll take the chest, all the way from the solar plexus up to the mid-chest, the chest in front, and just release and let the energy sink down. And now we're coming back to the midpoint in the back, so we're letting the energy release down through the solar plexus and through the midpoint of the back, touching the earth.

Then we'll come to the shoulder blades, points six and seven, and again, set your awareness within the shoulder blades. Breathe your awareness into the interior of the upper body, especially in front of the shoulder blades just inside your body, then below them, then to the sides. Feel the sensations, then the tension, and then relax.

Elbows, points eight and nine. (Make sure your hands are on your lower belly so the elbows are touching the earth.) Let the tension drain from the fingers, hands, wrists, lower arm down from the elbows. Shoulders, upper arms down through the elbows, into the earth. And now check the whole body, except for the head. Scan your awareness throughout the inside of your body. Are you able to let go any further? You are on a mission to detect where any additional tension is presenting itself. If you find any residual pockets of tension, connect with them and let go.

And then, finally, the head, point ten. Forehead, cheeks, nose. Teeth, jaws, tongue. Sides of the face, ears, scalp. Take time with each part. Breathing into each place, everything melts. Pay special attention to your face as a whole, for our face actually carries our whole ego identity and structure in it. It is said the Buddha's face was unimaginably beautiful to see and that is because his face, every aspect, surface and depth, was completely and utterly open, transparent, and relaxed. See what comes up for you when you do this part of the practice.

The eyes. Eye socket. The back of the eye, the optic nerve, a little down from center, all accessible when we put our attention there and relax. Again, the eye is a microcosm of the whole body and the tension we hold in our eyes is very much bound up in the tension we hold in our whole body. The eye can be the access point to the entire body. So relax the eye. Completely relax. You can close your eyes if you like. The upper lip. The lower lip. Let the whole face melt. Eyebrows. Let the face just become like putty, dissolving, softening, losing its shape completely. And then the top of the head. Let the energy just flow through the brain, out the back of the head, into the earth. We are so used to our head as the thinking place; in this practice, let it be a somatic, feeling place, a visceral reality, nothing more.

Now we are going to practice all Ten Points together. Let your awareness permeate your body and try to feel your body *as a whole*. To help you, try to breathe into all the pores of the skin of your entire body, all at once. See if you can find any other places that your body is calling to you to relax and release. And as you scan your body, notice your awareness. Can you sense a stillness in it? Attend to your body with a lot of energy and commitment and devotion. If your mind wanders at any point in the practice, which it is bound to do, just come back to your body; you're putting your whole attention in your body. You're feeling your body as a whole. Just being there. And keep relaxing. Keep letting go. It's almost as if your body is continually melting into the earth, under you. We're developing an attitude of intense listening to the body right now. Listening. Listening, relaxing, relaxing, letting go completely. Open, receptive to what may come back to you.

So we're looking to completely relax, even to the point of going to sleep. Just letting go of everything, and we're maintaining some level of attention during this process, of looking for places where we're holding on and letting go; and the body continues to offer these up. As long as we're willing to be present with our awareness, the body is continually showing us these places where we can release. So just look for those. And as you do this, you may find yourself wanting to adjust your hips on the floor, your legs, your arms, your upper body. Here as always, follow the promptings of your body. As we let go of the ego imposition and holding, we are able to find a natural alignment that is more consistent with our actual body rather than with anything we may be trying to do. So just make those adjustments, as you feel called to make them.

Moving into a Sitting Position

Take whatever time you would like, and just lie there feeling whatever you are feeling, exploring whatever is coming up. *And then, when you feel ready, you can sit back up.* As you resume a sitting posture, try to bring your present state of relaxation and somatic openness with you; be mindful of not freezing when you sit up. It is best if you can sit on something firm, with no back support, such as a meditation cushion, a meditation bench, or a flat chair with a firm bottom, in order to support you in making the transition from lying down to sitting up. This is a vulnerable and delicate moment, from the lying-down posture to the sitting up, and we want to bring with us as much of the somatic awareness we have just developed as we can; so we want to sit up very slowly, mindfully, and resist the temptation to lock up, space out, or shut down.

When you are in the sitting position, sit there for a few minutes and feel this out; be very attentive to what you're feeling right now. If you're feeling a little bit heavy or slightly deflated, this is a good sign. Just let it be that way. Explore it. Or you may be feeling more grounded. Initially it almost feels like depression, almost like what we're trying to run away from. And actually it *is* what we—or at least our ego—is trying to run away from. And yet, in the heaviness and weighted feeling of our somatic sense right now, our whole life and our whole future is present and brewing. So be with it, explore it and, if you can, take much confidence in it. If you notice an upswing in the volume of your thinking, you can regard the thoughts as tension, because they are. Compulsive thinking is a kind of tension. Just let it dissolve and flow down, just the way all the other tension does. So there's a constant steady stream downward, into the earth. You are already seeing what Ten Points practice sitting up might feel like.

When you feel familiar with Ten Points lying down, you can adapt this practice to sitting up and carry out the whole practice in a seated position, either in your meditation or just in the course of daily life—for example, sitting in a meeting or at the dinner table. No one around you need know. You may just seem a little more present and a little more interesting to them. In sitting-up Ten Points, the principles, steps, and procedures are the same although you will be making adjustments such as using whatever points of your body are in physical contact with the earth. Trust your experience and be willing to follow the lead of your body, whether lying down or sitting up, in terms of how it wants to use this practice as part of bringing you into its sphere and leading you on in your journey.

By way of conclusion, practice Ten Points with my guidance until you feel quite familiar with it and feel you have assimilated its basic steps. After you have done this, you can begin to do it on your own. This is an important step for, as each one's process and journey are ultimately quite individual, so is each person's practice of Ten Points and the other somatic protocols. When you have internalized the practice and are able to do it without my guidance, you are going to enter into an entirely new phase of Ten Points, making all sorts of discoveries and figuring out ways of carry out this protocol that will perfectly suit what, in your Soma and your journey, is being called for right now. Practicing on one's own or with a skilled teacher, the discoveries are in fact endless. I myself have done this practice thousands of times and invariably find it fresh, surprising, and new whenever I do it.

I have gone into a lot of detail in leading you through Ten Points because, as I have said, it is the basic practice that underlies and, in fact, includes all the other somatic protocols. If you are well practiced in Ten Points, all the other protocols will come to you much more easily and quickly. So it is worth your spending ample time with this particular practice.

6

Practice Two: Earth Descent

OVERVIEW

In making the somatic journey, after connecting with our own body as we began to do in Ten Points, the next most important thing is entering into a conscious relationship with the earth. When we enter the spiritual path, as mentioned, the scope of our emotional life greatly increases and intensifies. If we try to rely on ourselves alone—ourselves as a little, separate, fragile, vulnerable being—we will not be able to handle this increased range and intensity.

The only way we are going to be able to be with this increasing openness of our state of being is if we are experientially grounded in the earth beneath us, deeply rooted in her timeless, supporting, and immovable space. And this groundedness does have to be a matter of direct, personal—and relatively continuous—experience. As we practice and make the somatic journey, we need to feel like a mountain that rises up, but only out of a broad base that merges down into the infinite depth of the earth. Through Earth Descent practice, we begin to come into that kind of awareness, where the majority of our somatic "self-awareness" is in the earth below and the rest is up here on the surface, living out our sometimes stormy and uncertain life. Like the mountain, so profound and peaceful is our anchor in the earth beneath that the storms of our life can be experienced not only with no overwhelming alarm, but with appreciation of their power, majesty, and beauty.

In this practice, we are not leaving our body behind. We are not dissociating. Rather, we are opening and extending our somatic awareness downward, into the earth. This practice is going to challenge the way we habitually think of our awareness or consciousness as generally quite small, contained in our skull or, at most, circumscribed by the envelope of our skin. As the somatic practices quickly make clear, that limitation is an artificial construct. In fact, our awareness has no inbuilt or inherent limitation whatsoever. We begin to discover this perhaps surprising fact first in the Earth Descent.

Again, to emphasize, we are not leaving our body behind, but we're opening our body so that our sense of our somatic being is much, much vaster and includes the earth—is rooted in the earth. With this earth awareness, we discover that we needn't feel like a tumbleweed, blowing across the plains, uprooted and ungrounded, aimless, and disconnected. When we open our body and realize that our body is indeed rooted in, and in fact includes, the full depths of the earth, then we are connected with a much larger sense of Self, which includes the earth.

In this practice, we are not looking at the earth from the outside. In an earlier section, in reference to how we are going to know the body, I mentioned that we are not considering it as an external observer might, but rather we are entering into it with our awareness and exploring it from the inside, viewing it from within, a process called interoception. We are going to do the same thing with the earth. This may sound implausible in the telling, but in practice the experience of it comes quite naturally. We have already had some taste of this in Ten Points practice. We are going to take the same approach in Earth Descent, develop the same interoception. This is possible because, ultimately, the impression that the earth is separate from our body is a conceptual overlay on a reality that is actually quite different. In fact, the earth is not in any definitive way something separate from our own felt and sensed state of being. The earth is a more extensive dimension, discovered experientially, of our own somatic being.

In this practice, I am asking you to set aside everything you may have learned about the geological structure and composition of the earth. Here we are taking a completely different approach. I am asking you to begin with the interior, somatic awareness of your body that you met in Ten Points and then to open and extend that very same somatic awareness downward into the earth.

In the beginning, this is likely to be a challenging concept. We may feel that extending cranial awareness into the rest of the body is plausible—"At least it is *my* awareness coming into presence in *my* body"—but doing the same thing with the earth? However, I am suggesting a different way of knowing. If we accept the possibility that our awareness has no boundaries—a possibility I hope will shortly be experientially sensed—then just as we know our body from the inside, so we can know the earth from the inside, too. Once we extend our awareness into the earth, we are already viewing it from within itself; we are knowing it from the inside. Let me just say it: we are knowing the earth as she knows herself. This is what happens when mothers and infants entrain, and that process is exactly what is happening here. We are entraining with the earth.

We are going to begin this practice with the same lying-down posture we used for Ten Points: on our back, knees up, feet flat on the floor, rug, or cushion, hands crossed over the lower belly. In Ten Points, we went through a process of connecting with each part of our body beginning with the feet, feeling the physical sensations in each place, noticing the tension, and releasing the tension down into the earth. In the Earth Descent, we are going to begin where Ten Points left off; we will start by feeling our body, but this time as a whole, sensing first the overall sensations of our body as a totality, then feeling all at once all the body's myriad tensions—the dammed-up life force or energy—and releasing this down into the earth. In Earth Descent, though, we are going to follow the flow of this tension/energy down into the earth. More precisely, we are going to use the downward flow of energy as a vehicle to extend our somatic awareness and open downward, deeper and deeper into the earth.

THE PRACTICE

Let's use the cycle of the in-breath and out-breath as an aid. On the in-breath, just be in your body and feel it as a whole. Now sense whatever tension is presenting itself. On the out-breath, release the tension down into the earth. Do this a few times until you feel comfortable with the cycle, "in-breath feel the tension, out-breath release downward." Next, feel the tension on the in-breath, and on the out-breath release and extend your awareness beneath you about two feet. Do this a few times; on the next out-breath, extend your awareness down three feet. Then, on the next out breath, extend downward four feet, and open downward another foot with each successive breath until you are extending downward to ten feet.

In the beginning, it is appropriate to go very slowly with Earth Descent. In this guided practice, I am going to take you through the main phases of the entire process. However, if you begin to feel apprehensive, then just rest where you are, without necessarily trying to go any further. In fact, in your first several sessions of Earth Descent, just explore as far as feels right to you. As long as you stay in control of the practice and your own experience of it, in each practice session you will begin from a place of felt safety and security, and this is important. Pushing beyond that zone of somatic "okayness" is counterproductive and will set up unconscious patterns of resistance. The body will let you know just how far is right; it is only the spiritually ambitious ego that would like to override the body's wisdom and push on.

On your next out-breath, extend downward to ten feet but, on the in-breath, leave the outer margin of your somatic awareness down at ten feet. On the next out-breath extend another ten feet downward so you are open to twenty feet beneath you. Then, on the in-breath again leaving your awareness at twenty feet, extend down another ten feet and keep extending downward another ten feet, then increase to twenty feet, then to fifty feet on each out-breath. Then you can extend downward at increments of a hundred, five hundred, a thousand feet. Explore your own inner feel of how to move downward, in what increments and at what speed. At some point, you may wish to leave the breath aside and simply focus on descending.

As you extend downward, you are likely to meet resistance within yourself. You may start to think the earth is solid; you may feel obstacles of all sorts, thoughts, doubts, even see images of walls and barriers. As each of these comes into view, remember that you are meeting your own assumptions and preconceptions. These are just self-created barriers; in the earth's space, there are no impediments whatsoever. Just let them go and keep opening your somatic awareness downward, ever deeper into the earth. Notice fear, notice hesitation, notice the way in which we artificially limit our awareness going down. There is part of us that wants to hang on for dear life to a restricted sense of ourselves. Letting go of the hesitation and the fear, just keep extending downward. If you do begin to feel that it is a little too much, a little too overwhelming, just relax and back up, come up to a level where it feels okay. The further steps I am about to describe may take many iterations of the practice over a long period to be experienced with clarity and confidence—perhaps weeks, months, or even longer. However, if you go gently, the full experience of Earth Descent will eventually be yours.

EARTH DESCENT PRACTICE.

To continue, at a certain point, you can let go of the idea of increments entirely and just imagine that your awareness is extending and opening downward in a steady way, like a snowflake falling through the air or, more quickly, like a stone dropped into a bottomless well. As you descend, have the feeling of your somatic awareness not only going down but also going out to the sides; so the overall feel is that your awareness is becoming more and more vast beneath you.

Keep the feeling that it is your own body, your somatic being, that is opening deeper and deeper discovering new dimensions of itself. Let the leading edge of your somatic awareness extend downward faster and faster. And now open all the way down; see if you can just let go completely into the fathomless depth. Let the bottom fall out. Just extend and then, abruptly, *open to infinity under you.* So now a sense that the depth is infinite—it has no end—and opening to that endless depth . . . This can become a tangible, direct, personal—and visceral, bodily—experience.

It's now an utter, unconditional opening on our part. Feel the infinite depth of your body's own space. Notice that there is no break between our awareness of our body and the awareness of the earth—it's one continuous experience of primordial being. It's as if the body itself is receiving, is participating in, *is* in fact the experience of this infinite depth of the earth. Obviously, at this point we have moved beyond any idea of the earth as a physical object with definite boundaries; the earth is now functioning as a gate to the experience of the infinity of space as the actual somatic scope of our body.

In order to develop the practice further, now notice the space in your somatic being as it is open and inclusive of the vastness of the earth. See how that makes you feel. As you extend and open downward, also notice the *quality* of the space of the earth beneath. Does it feel warm? Welcoming? Nurturing? Safe? As you descend, do you feel as if you were coming home? Is there an increasingly primordial feel to this much vaster and deeper scope of your body? Does the space feel healing? These kinds of questions are deliberately leading, used in the Tibetan tradition to direct our attention to things we might not otherwise notice.

Now returning to your circumscribed body on the surface of the earth, bounded by the envelope of your skin, see if you can allow the energy of the earth into any place in your body or your psyche that feels compromised, shut off, or in need of healing. In fact, you have the ability to direct the energy of the earth to those places. If your heart is sore and wounded, then open your heart and receive the healing energy of the earth. . . . The more present you can be, the more blissful the earth's love—and the more healing occurs.

You can keep going with this practice, going deeper and deeper and exploring the feel of the body/earth space as long as you like. Enjoy the experiences that open up, of peace and ease, of being held, nurtured, and protected, of profound healing. Savor the sense of relaxation and openness when we are so deeply connected with and at one with the earth. The growing sense that we are discovering our true home and foundation is going to provide a contentment, a sense of well-being, a somatic confidence, and a grounding that will be essential to our further journey.

This Earth Descent is best learned and explored lying down, but then it can be practiced in a sitting-up position. Particularly when we are engaged in sitting meditation, the somatic awareness developed through the Earth Descent is a most important dimension of the meditation posture. As we meditate, we are thus able to have the feeling of our awareness deeply rooted in the infinite depth of the earth and held within her warm, nurturing, protected space. Meditation practiced with this deep rooting in the earth has a very different feel and outcome from anything we could do without this grounding.

The sitting-up practice of the Earth Descent is just the same as the lying-down practice, except for one detail. As you descend into the earth, you breathe up from the deepest point your somatic awareness has reached as a way to connect your body and your practice with that depth. You bring the breath up, through your perineum, and into your body. So on every out-breath, you open your Soma to a particular depth; on the in-breath, you breathe up into your body from that place. On the next out-breath, you open your somatic space deeper and then breathe up from that place, always through your perineum. Even when dropping to infinity, you still imagine you are open to and breathing up from that infinite depth, drawing the space up from that place, into your body on the surface.

7

Practice Three: Yin Breathing

In Ten Points, we began exploring our body, learning to feel its sensations and then its tension. Through gradually relaxing our places of holding, we began to see what it might mean to experience our body without interference. In Earth Descent, we saw that when we look directly, we find no strict demarcation between the interior space of the body and the space beyond, in the earth; our awareness just seems to extend indefinitely beyond the body.

In the next practice, Yin Breathing, we are going to take a closer look at the experience of space *within* our body. The term "yin" is Taoist, referring to feminine space, feminine reality, in contrast to "yang," the masculine principle or reality. We are not talking primarily here about concepts of human gender but instead about basic, experiential principles of polarity that exist throughout our entire experience: night and day, health and sickness, light and dark, life and death, male and female—throughout all the realms of animal and plant life and so on. Within the human body, the

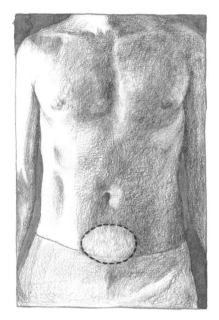

THE APPROXIMATE LOCATION OF THE DAN T'IEN.

place of yin is in the lower belly, approximately a couple of inches below the navel and in about the middle of the body. This place is extremely important in Chan and Zen meditation, where it is called the *hara,* and in Tibetan tantra, where is it known as the secret center.

In Taoist meditation, this place in the lower belly is known as the lower *dan t'ien.* The lower dan t'ien is not defined very strictly in terms of shape or size or even precise location, since the experience of it will vary from person to person and from one practice session to another even with the same individual.[1] However, initially as a helpful entry, it can be thought of as having a roughly egg shape, perhaps as small as a hen's egg or larger like a goose egg. Sometimes it is felt right in the middle of the body between front and back; other times, it can be felt more toward the back or more toward the front.

The lower dan t'ien plays a unique role within the human body and in Somatic Meditation. To put it in a nutshell, within the human body, it is a kind of basic Source. It represents the most primordial and most complete of all the somatic spaces in and through our body—and, as we shall see, there are many such spaces to discover. Moreover, the lower dan t'ien provides access to something much, much vaster that cannot be contained by our body at all. By breathing into the lower dan t'ien, we are able to find this secret access. The space in the lower dan t'ien, within our body, is the inner expression of the fundamental space of the cosmos, the original womb out of which all energy and life arise. It is the microcosmic expression of the same limitless reality we meet "outside" in the earth at its infinite depth (the macrocosm). By tapping into the lower dan t'ien, we are able to tap into the primal, unformed energy of the universe itself (known as *huntun,* or chaos, in Taoism[2]). By breathing into the lower dan t'ien, in a purely somatic way, we will be able to contact the most complete and primordial space of our human body, the transmitter from beyond time and space of the life force—our life force—that continually arises from that space. If you want to know, right now, who you most fundamentally are and where you came from, here it is, available for you to experience directly.

As an analogy, I might mention the quantum emptiness of the universe, discussed in astrophysics and quantum mechanics, that is thought to underlie the universe and out of which, it is believed, all existing energy and matter arose in the so-called big bang and out of which, moment by moment, energy and matter continue to be born. But I don't think this is just an analogy: I would suggest that the space of the lower dan t'ien *is* the quantum emptiness of the cosmos (again, macrocosm), as experienced in the human body (microcosm), and it continually gives birth to the energy of our life on the microcosmic level. But, importantly, you will need to test these suggestions in your own practice, seeing what you find and if they make sense.

THE PRACTICE

As usual, we are going to begin by learning this practice lying down, and then we will bring it up into a sitting position. So please take the customary lying-down position, on your back, knees up, perhaps tied with something, feet flat on the floor, hands crossed over the lower belly, left hand under the right. Make whatever micro-adjustments you need to so that you are completely relaxed in this position. Here, in particular, loose clothing is important so that your lower belly feels easy, free, and open.

The practice instructions are simple compared to the previous two practices. As you are lying there, try to feel the place of the lower dan t'ien, or hara, the place of yin. In the beginning, you probably won't have any direct experience of it; you will need to begin by imagining where it might be and then trying to feel.

Next, begin breathing into the lower dan t'ien or into the place you think or sense it might be. Again, use your imagination: visualize this space and imagine that you are breathing right into the center of it. We are not bringing our breath in through our nostrils or down through our airways or even trying to breathe in from the outside at all. We are simply imagining the center of the space and attempting to breathe directly into that place. Use your physical breath as an aid. On the in-breath, just visualize you are breathing right into that point. As you are doing this, try to get the feeling of opening up the space in the lower belly: opening, opening, opening.

A good place to begin is to imagine that your lower belly is like a balloon: on the in-breath, you imagine the balloon is inflating; on the out-breath, imagine it is somewhat deflating. On the in-breath, you feel yourself breathing right into that place; on the out-breath, you just imagine the balloon deflating—you don't worry about where the breath goes. Use this visualization for a while until it feels easy and continuous. It may take many tries before you feel you are catching on. Try to keep your attention on the space and within it at its very center, breathing into it and continually opening it up. As you continue, try to be more and more focused right in the center and more present to it.

When the balloon visualization begins to feel doable—it doesn't have to be perfect!—then shift your attention to the point in the middle of the balloon that you are breathing into. Try to be really there, just breathing into that point and, as you do this, relax and let go of the balloon imagery.

Perhaps surprisingly, you may be able to actually feel the freshness and coolness and purity of the breath as you breathe in to that point. If so, be with that sensation and use it to help you stay within the lower belly space. At a certain point, you can relax your focus on the point in the center and just experience the literal space of the lower dan t'ien; it will become so clear and obvious, and compelling, you will wonder how in the world you were not previously aware of it and how it could have taken you so long in the practice to feel it.

In Yin Breathing, we are roaming on the boundary between consciousness (the ego domain) and the unconscious (the deep Soma). Don't expect your awareness within the yin space necessarily to look the same or have the same qualities as the awareness of the ego consciousness that you are accustomed to. You may find your mind dark or murky, or shifting, or swimmy. Sometimes the awareness is amazingly soft, subtle, and tender. Or it may feel quite fluid and watery. Or sometimes crystal clear. Sometimes, again, it may feel stunningly empty. You may sometimes find yourself drifting toward sleep, with various images and dreamlike experiences moving in and out. You may wonder whether you are actually being aware at all. You may even drift into sleep for a while. None of this is a problem; it is actually part of the evolving practice. The most important thing is to try to register whatever happens, no matter what state of mind you may be in. Constantly have the curiosity to ask yourself, What is going on here? What am I sensing or feeling? What is this, right now? Treat it as an adventure into an unknown land, for that it exactly what it is. You will learn things in the practice, but since the kind of learning is generally so unfamiliar, it may take time to realize what is going on. And, in the beginning, you may not remember very much.

How should we work with distraction? Here is the technique I propose: as the yin space begins to open up for you, dissolve everything into it on the in-breath. Whatever's going on with you—thinking, feeling, physical sensations, feeling sick, feeling hungry, whatever it may be—everything dissolves on the in-breath into the yin space. The whole body and everything going on within it relaxes and dissolves into the lower belly on the in-breath. Allow a feeling of folding your entire body into the yin space. In this way, the energy of the distraction actually fuels the practice and enhances our presence within the lower dan t'ien.

The Yin Breathing practice is going to take time to develop. When I first began exploring it, sometimes it took forty-five minutes or more for something to happen. It is fine if you don't have that much time; everything counts and even a minute of practice will lead you toward your goal. But know that you will likely need to spend some serious time with Yin Breathing to actually get the feeling of it and experientially discover what is there for you. Keep in mind that we are talking about connecting with our Source; we are talking about touching the basic, quantum realities of the universe in our body; it is worth the effort!

As you continue with the practice, at a certain point you may find that you are becoming ever so much more peaceful. You are beginning to tap into the yin space, which is utter peace itself. Over the course of your practice, you may discover other qualities: simplicity, purity, clarity, warmth, protection, nourishment, and healing. To say again, the yin space is the cosmic space of the earth as it appears in our body. Rest there; luxuriate; whatever feelings of well-being and bliss may come your way, enjoy them. But don't push it: when things don't come, let it be; when things do come, no big deal—don't make anything out of them.

Later in the practice, you may make some further discoveries. Perhaps at some point there won't be any "you" breathing; there will just be the breathing itself. Just that freshness, that coolness, that feeling of the breath emptying into that soothing place. And perhaps you will suddenly realize that you can't find the edges of the yin space at all; abruptly, it may have no shape or limits and you may find yourself not in a space in the body but just in primordial space, period. No sense of boundary or reference point. It will feel like—because it is—the fundamental space of the endless universe. It feels just like the infinitude we experience in the Earth Descent, and that is because, in fact, they are the same reality, entered by us through different gates. Again, just be with it without judgment or comment. But it certainly gives you a lot to think about later.

Give yourself plenty of time to explore the practice and become familiar with it in the lying-down position. Beyond your formal sessions of practice, you can do this anytime you are lying down; it is especially interesting to do at night, when you are going to sleep or when you wake up in the middle of the night. It is truly a miraculous gate into the primordial, and sometimes when we are hovering near sleep, it can open up in unique ways.

When you feel ready, you can begin to explore the Yin Breathing practice in a sitting-up posture. You can use it very fruitfully in meditation practice. In our practicing lineage, it is breathing into the lower dan t'ien that is the main breath technique rather than putting attention at the tip of the nose. As you meditate, you simply breathe into the lower dan t'ien, as we have just done, and explore how the experience, the space, and your awareness evolve. You can also do the Yin Breathing anytime, in any situation. It is a wonderful way to bring oneself back, to reconnect with the primordial, to reboot our system, so to speak, and begin anew from there.

8

Practice Four:
Coming into the Central Channel

As I've been saying, the body that we habitually think we have is a conceptual construct, an overlay on something else. That "something else" is our actual body: it is what we see when we view it through the lens of direct, nonconceptual experience, available when we engage in the inner journey of the interoception, of inner sensing and feeling.

In the first three practices, we have already had quite a bit of experience of this real, actual body of ours. In Yin Breathing, in particular, we discovered that when we inspect our lower belly, far from finding it stuffed full of our digestive apparatus and other organs, when viewed in our direct experience, it holds a profound and completely open space. So in this case, the lower belly of the conceptual body is what we think is there; the lower belly of our true, directly experienced body is this primordial space.

So within the yin space of the lower belly we discover the empty, open, primordial space of our body, where the quantum emptiness of the cosmos manifests itself. The lower belly may be the place where this primal space is most accessible, but it is not the only place. In fact, there are many other spaces, the most important of which you will be introduced to and practice within the course of this book. All of the spaces we will find are vulnerable points in our conceptualized body. This means that when we attend to these vulnerable points, we can see through the conceptually fabricated overlay quite easily to what lies on the other side: that is, to our actual body.

The central channel is another one of these places where the primal space can be met and experienced. As with the yin space, the central channel has a special importance in the traditions mentioned and others, especially Tibetan tantra, Chan and Zen, Hindu yoga, and Taoist meditation. In terms of its structure, the central channel lies along our spinal column, but just inside our body. (See figures on p. 75.) It is usually visualized as a kind of tube, extending from the perineum all the way up to the top of the head. The precise visualization varies, depending on how it is being used. Though in some cases it is seen as going over the top of the head and down to the nostrils in front, in our case it stops at the top of the head. The diameter of the central channel varies, again depending on the specific tradition and the uses to which it is being put. For our purposes, you can visualize it as about half an inch in diameter up to an inch. As you do the practice, see what feels right to you.

THE PRACTICE

The Central Channel practice is one of the few body work protocols that we need to learn sitting up. In fact, nearly all the use we will make of it will be in the sitting-up position. It can, occasionally be done lying down, but that is much more difficult and will only be possible once we are thoroughly familiar with the sitting-up version. We also need to learn and mostly practice

Central Channel in meditation posture with no back support. This is because only in this way will the inner space of the central channel be fully accessible and unimpeded. And when we practice meditation, we are going to need the central channel to be the energetic and spatial core of our meditation posture.

There are three options for how you can sit in meditation posture for this practice: cross-legged on a firm cushion, in the usual Zen and Tibetan style; knees together with feet behind you, sitting on your feet (perhaps lifted slightly by a bench, blanket, or cushion under your buttocks), Japanese *seiza* style; or on a meditation bench or chair with a firm seat, as long as you are able to sit upright without leaning against the chair back. If you are injured and need to lean against a chair back or other support, you can do so and will still be able to do the practice. It is important to find the right position, one that allows both physical uprightness as well as physical ease and relaxation. For Central Channel practice, whichever posture you pick, it is important to be able to feel your spine being aligned, open, and relaxed. The interoceptive experience needs to be, in the words of the ancient Chan master Hongzhi, "dignified and upright" and "independent."[1] This will provide greatest access to the practice.

Let's begin our Central Channel practice with sitting-up Yin Breathing. If you are not sufficiently familiar with that practice to do it from memory, consult the instructions. Otherwise, just begin to breathe into your lower belly. Take some time, open up the space, and feel your breath entering and dissolving into the lower dan t'ien. Now we are going to use the breath to gradually open the yin space into the central channel, extending upward increment by increment, until the entire central channel is inflated, so to speak, with the space of the lower dan t'ien. In the beginning, this visualization may seem somewhat artificial. However, because you are imagining something that is actually really in our nonconceptualized body—that is, our real body—at a certain point you will feel it vividly for yourself.

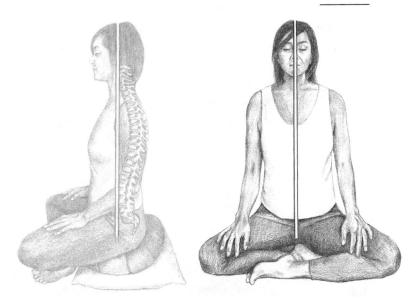

THE CENTRAL CHANNEL, VIEWED FROM THE SIDE AND FRONT.

The entry point of the central channel—where we are going to be drawing the breath into it—is about three or four inches below the navel and at the back of the body, right in front of the sacrum. This will feel like the back part of the lower dan t'ien. Begin by breathing into this place. Keep breathing and paying attention to your experience of bringing the breath into this place. Continuing to breathe, see if any one spot in particular stands out as feeling like a gate or a hole. This gate or hole is one of the particularly vulnerable places in our conceptualized body, our solidified version of our body, that I have been talking about.

Breathe into this place, or visualize that you are breathing into this place. Imagine that, as you do so, you are opening the space of the lower dan t'ien into that hole. Now visualize that, breath by breath, you are very slowly, incrementally, opening and extending the space of the lower dan t'ien up the central channel. With each breath, bring the breath up higher, perhaps a half inch or so; try to be very present and fully attentive as you do. Make sure you remain grounded in the space of the lower dan t'ien so that you are not losing your anchor there; but at the same time you are opening the breath—the space, the awareness, for they are ultimately all the same—up and up and up.

Keep opening the breath up through this tube of the central channel. Imagine that you are extending a kind of corridor or column of space up, as if it were in the tube shape. Continue to stay connected with the lower dan t'ien, and keep extending the breath up: up the back of the lower belly, past the navel, the solar plexus, behind the base of the throat, behind the vocal cords, up behind the palate, up inside the head but toward the back, to the occiput (the little bump on the back of your head), up to top of the head. Come to the top, but no further; we do not want to exit the body through the top of the head. Now have the feeling of laying your awareness along the entire extent of the central channel, from the space in the lower dan t'ien up to the top of the head. We might think that to be aware of space in the body, we have to pay attention to one particular location, but such is not the case. Once we get used to the idea, we can lay our awareness along this entire corridor of space and feel the whole thing, all at once. Work at this and don't be discouraged if this kind of less-pinpointed awareness takes time to develop. We are developing a capacity here that looks forward. In the next practice, we will develop the ability to be present to the entire body all at once, something we touched on briefly in the Ten Points practice.

Ask yourself, What is the quality of space within the central channel? Does it feel clogged or compromised in any way? If so, have the feeling of letting go of whatever obstructions you feel. You may want to wiggle your alignment around a little to ease whatever kinks or tensions you are feeling. Empty out, empty, empty, let go; have the feeling of opening the space and clearing it. As you do so, see if you can tune in to its empty, open, immaculate quality. Let go into this space and sense it as the basic core of your being, for that is what it is. Take as much time as you need to feel what this is like; enjoy the openness, the freedom, and the ease that it brings to your whole body. It may take time to develop this as a definite and repeatable experience, but given practice, it will come.

When we are abiding within the immaculate space either of the lower dan t'ien or the central channel, we are resting within what is called the unborn nature, the unconditioned awareness that is the ground of our being. In Buddhism, this is known as the buddha nature. Once we are familiar with this practice, whenever we get lost, in whatever circumstance or situation, no matter how disconcerting, confusing, or chaotic, we can abruptly reenter the central channel and reconnect with our primordial being. Trungpa Rinpoche called this move "back to square one." Then, with nobody in our immediate environment having any idea of what we are doing, we can turn our attention back toward whatever is going on, but from a very different place. Rooted in the unborn, all kinds of previously unseen possibilities will be there for us.

9

Practice Five:
Whole Body Breathing and Rooting

OVERVIEW

Up until this point, we have been working individually with various aspects of the body and the somatic process: we have connected with the body, identifying and releasing tension in Ten Points practice; developed grounding and somatic confidence in Earth Descent practice; discovered the most fundamental inner space of the body in the lower belly in Yin Breathing practice; and explored how this basic inner space provides the experiential core of our being in the Central Channel practice. As suggested in its name, Whole Body Breathing is the first practice devoted exclusively to taking the body as a whole as our focus of awareness. In this practice, we are going to breathe into our body through all of our pores at once; in that sense, the practice has a close relationship to Ten Points. But it takes much further the kind of global awareness we touched upon briefly at the end of Ten Points, further extending, refining, and enhancing the experience of the interior space of the body of the Yin Breathing and Central Channel practices.

In Whole Body Breathing, by breathing in through all of the pores of our body and into its innermost regions, all at once, we are going to be further developing a global feeling of the body from the inside. As we shall presently see, inseparable from the breath is the feeling of the energy of the life force and of awareness. So when you are breathing in through your pores, you have a feeling of bringing not only breath but also energy, light, and awareness into your body. You have a sense of filling up with this breath/energy/light/awareness, as if you were pouring water into your body and completely filling up the envelope of your skin, including every nook and cranny. In this practice, there is no focusing or privileging of any one part of the body over another; every aspect is felt equally as a part of the whole, both surface and depth, down to the cells. In the past, I have sometimes used the term "cellular breathing," referring to the fact that through it, we are seeking to awaken the awareness of the very cells themselves. In fact, in the practice, we may begin to find an extraordinarily subtle sense where it feels that our cells have come alive and have "lit up," so to speak.[1]

Whole Body Breathing develops a level of intense, interior, global somatic presence that we have not yet experienced. As we shall see, it will be extremely useful in any subsequent stages of the embodying processes in meditation, compassion work, or Tibetan Vajrayana practice. Beyond this, Whole Body Breathing is uniquely valuable for its ability to bring us into our entire body in this very direct and immediate way, even when we may be feeling quite disconnected and disembodied. This practice can also be used to support healing in injury or illness, since it is a way to augment oxygenation, nourishment, energy, and enhanced neurological function and growth to various affected areas of the body to promote and speed healing.

THE PRACTICE

Please take the lying-down position, on your back, feet flat on the floor, knees up, perhaps with a yoga strap around your legs (just above the knee for maximum stability and relaxation in your psoas muscles, lower back, and pelvis). Cross your hands over the lower belly to augment the experience of the energy there, the qi or prana, and hence to enhance your somatic awareness.

Begin with an abbreviated Ten Points practice. First feel the physical sensations of your body; you might begin with your feet and then slowly sweep your attention upward, including more and more of your body, to your head. Now feel the sensations of your body as a whole. Spend some time here, opening to the full sensory experience of your body: physical, energetic, emotional. Just be with it and take it in. Notice what comes forward from this holistic field toward your consciousness.

Next, breathing in through all your pores, be present in your body, as a whole and all at once, and attend to wherever you feel tension. Be within your body as a vast and open field, and be roaming around, noticing places that stand out with tension of any sort. You may notice one part, now another, then larger areas, perhaps even your body as a whole. Just as in the last stage of Ten Points practice, wherever there is tension in your body, try breathing into it, and invite release; try to let it melt and dissolve down, as in Earth Descent practice; let go and let the downward flow connect you energetically with the earth.

Now begin to breathe in more intently through all the pores of your body. At first, imagine that you are breathing in just the air. On your in-breath, feel you are inhaling into your body through all your pores at once; the pores *do* breathe, so this is not pure imagination. In fact, if you attend closely, on your in-breath, you may be able to feel the air coming in through the pores; it will generally be a slightly cool, fresh feeling. Imagine your body filling up with the refreshing air and its life-giving oxygen. See if you can sense your body responding positively, brightening, with uplift, to the inflow of the delicious, oxygen-laden air. Do this for a few minutes, until the experience becomes real and you actually feel it in your body.

Next, imagine that inseparable from the breath you are breathing in is the energy of life, the life force itself, and imagine that as you breathe in, your body is filling with this energy so that your body comes further to life. Again, do this for a few minutes until you experience it somatically. Next, imagine you are breathing in awareness itself, which is the essence of the breath and the life force. And finally, image you are breathing in light. Now imagine that your body is filling up with awareness and light.

Continue breathing in, in this way through all your pores. Feel what it is like as you continue with the practice; try especially to breathe into areas that feel dark or numb or deflated. Imagine that the more you are breathing in through all your pores, the more your body, bounded by the envelope of your skin, is being filled with awareness and light; it is becoming a body of openness, awareness, and luminosity, a body you can feel as a whole, in its totality.

As you continue breathing in like this, try to come into your body with greater and greater intent, attention, focus, and presence. You are coming into your body more fully, more intensely, more brightly, more exuberantly, exclusively to the point where you are letting your awareness of anything else, anything outside, drop away. You are completely within your body now, your body is one of awareness and light, and there isn't anything else.

The Rooting Practice

We are now going to turn to the Rooting practice, which is an enhancement or further refinement and deepening of Whole Body Breathing. Continuing with Whole Body Breathing, visualize that the breath/life force/awareness/light that is coming in through your pores is coming to each cell in your body. Try to feel into your body down to this level of subtlety. Do that until you have a global sense of all your cells receiving the breath. Feel that this breath, inseparable from energy and awareness, is landing in each cell and try to feel how each of your cells is receiving it, and how each of your cells feels about it. Although the refinement of cellular awareness called for here may seem a bit far-fetched at first, since Candace Pert's work on the molecules of emotion, we have external, experimental evidence that the cells are aware and do feel;[2] and this practice invites us to discover that fact for ourselves, experientially. Make sure you spend enough time with this part of the practice, especially in the beginning, so that you have some actual somatic experience. Remember, we are developing capacity here that will serve us well from now on in every aspect of our spiritual practice and life.

Next, imagine that you are breathing the breath/life force/awareness/light that is now so abundant in your cells up from those cells into your torso, up to the mid-chest area, where you can most fully and precisely experience it, not just physically and energetically, but on a subtle feeling level as well. You are trying to breathe up what the cells know, what *they* feel. So you are trying to take into your somatic consciousness what each cell has for you and wants to communicate; you are feeling into those cells individually but also with all of them included in one whole, somatic experience, and you are breathing up their information, what they hold and what they are experiencing, their feeling of breath/life force/awareness/light, up into your mid-chest. This does indeed have the feel of rooting—hence the name of the practice—that your embodied, conscious experience is deeply rooted all the way down to—and in—your cells.

Because it is through the cells that we connect and commune with the entire universe, the rooting we are doing here has a feeling of being rooted in—dare I say—the cosmic Totality, reality itself. It's essential to emphasize, once again, that we are not talking theory here; I am pointing you toward a concrete, tangible, personal experience. It is only on this level that the Rooting practice, like all of the other protocols, can possibly make any sense. And when we know in this experiential way, no other sense is needed or wanted, though we might want to sing about it or dance or make love to our world.

Practice Whole Body Breathing and its Rooting Enhancement for a while, until you feel fairly familiar and easy with it. Then you can begin to practice it in the sitting-up meditation posture. It is the same practice sitting up as lying down. Unlike some of the other somatic protocols, once you learn it in the lying-down position, this practice is actually more accessible in the sitting-up position and easier to carry out in that way. Do it sitting up and find your way into its comfort and ease. Over time, it brings a bodily feel of relaxation, naturalness, and well-being that you will greatly appreciate.

In the practice of Whole Body Breathing with the Rooting Enhancement, we are trying to develop a greater and greater feeling of being within our body, a greater and more comprehensive sense of somatic presence, beingness, and interior awareness. We just keep making it brighter and brighter, more and more intense. Continue with this practice for a while; see how fully and exclusively you can be within this body of awareness and light that you are developing.

A Variant of Whole Body Breathing: Nighttime Practice

At this point, I want to show you a variant of Whole Body Breathing that you can do at night, lying in bed, before you go to sleep, or if you wake up in the middle of the night. It can be especially helpful if you suffer from insomnia. This Nighttime practice begins as you are lying in bed, eyes closed, and in a comfortable position; now you are going to begin to breathe in through all the pores of your skin as in the Rooting practice above. This version of the practice is simpler than the full one just described, because you are just bringing in the breath and not going through the other steps.

As you begin to breathe in through all your pores, your attention wants already to be within your body. Feel the inner space of your body, the darkness of it, and feel into it and through it, as if your awareness is extending and expanding throughout the entire inner territory of your body. It may take a little while to develop this sense, especially in the beginning when you are first doing it.

Now begin breathing in a more intentional or directed way into your Soma's interior darkness. Here we are deliberately looking for the qualities of the somatic space, in the different regions. Are there places that feel rather open? Bring the breath through them. Are there other places that seem a little clogged or insentient? Draw the breath into them in a very intentional way until you feel your awareness arriving there. Are there places of physical restriction, achiness, or fatigue? Bring the breath right to them. In addition to what is mentioned here, there are many, many other kinds of similar sensations—some perhaps extraordinarily refined, maybe even an infinite number of them—that you will find in this Nighttime practice. In each case draw your breath into those sensations, let the breath flow through them, and try to let your awareness melt into them.

So here you are, in the middle of the night, getting in some practice time. Even if on this occasion you go back to sleep quickly and easily, the practice will deepen your sleep after you do it and facilitate a kind of underlying somatic awareness that you may find reverberating subtly throughout your morning practice and your day.

I mentioned that insomnia can be addressed through this protocol; in fact Whole Body Breathing can be a very interesting and impactful practice if you suffer from insomnia or even if occasionally you wake up in the middle of the night vexed by some issue or problem and have trouble going back to sleep. If you are doing this practice to address insomnia or sleeplessness, as your first step, take a look at your lifestyle and see if that is contributing to your difficulty in sleeping. I am not a sleep therapist, but over the years I have identified several factors that, at least for me, lead to sleep problems. At the risk of sounding like Dear Abby or your mother, I want to mention a few here.

Some obvious points: if you have consumed caffeine or other stimulants too near to bedtime, Whole Body Breathing will work, but it is obviously going to take more time and be a lot more difficult. Electronic devices similarly create a tremendous amount of somatic agitation and subliminal anxiety and these, I am sorry to say, include pretty much everything electronic: television, being on a computer, playing electronic games, peering into any electronic screen—TV is one of the worst—even talking on a cell phone or texting, when engaged in too close to sleeping, have all been shown to interfere with sound sleep—or, for some of us, sleeping at all. For me, the cutoff is about three to four hours before going to sleep. That sounds like a lot, particularly in light of the demands of our modern society; however, bad news as this may be, at least for me, that seems to be a nonnegotiable reality. Sound, deep sleep is not something you can play around with and ignore for very long without all kinds of physical and psychological problems.

Beyond this, insomnia is often fueled by the general stress level of modern life, which is chronically and toxically high for most of us. Extreme stress not only interferes with the well-being brought about by wholesome sleep, it also makes it very difficult to settle into the somatic stillness and peace that is so important— and felt as so fulfilling—on the meditative journey.

That said, let's address the sleepless situation and see how Whole Body Breathing might help to remedy it. Let's say that you cannot get to sleep or you have awakened and cannot get back to sleep, so you are just lying there in bed, thinking or counting sheep or whatever you do. Now you can turn to your Whole Body Breathing. To begin with, you are going to have to get out of your head, with all of its thinking and stories and grinding away, which is so often a major player in insomnia. We are using this practice here to drop under all of that. If you also feel anxiety or some other strong affect running amok, you are going to have to drop under that, too. If you simply feel very strong energy, like electricity, running through you, you are going to have to drop under that as well. You are using this practice, first, to come into your body. If you are very "wired," as we might say, this is going to take some time. Don't worry, you've got plenty of time—maybe the whole night. Just stick with it. Eventually, you will arrive in your body. You will just be in a feeling and a sensing state, without much else. Next, begin to bring the breath into the interior space, as described above. Again, this may take time, but you are developing a skill that will grow the more you do it and that in the long run may help you a great deal. Think of it this way: you are developing your Somatic Meditation practice and you are also aiming to get back to sleep—so killing two birds with one stone, so to speak. So don't become too discouraged.

In trying to sleep or go back to sleep, your somatic fatigue will be your most important ally. Anytime you do this practice, even if you want to do it during the day to take a nap, whether you would *say* or *think* you are tired or not, there are going to be interior areas that feel enormously fatigued. At first, you may be completely unaware of these places. Our body and various locales with in it—which will differ for each of us—are at all times carrying an enormous physical and psychological load, though generally we are completely unconscious of the resulting fatigue and sinking, heavy tiredness that is there, in our body. Even in chronic sleeplessness, we are often unaware of this deepest level of fatigue. But now let's use it. Now we are going to look for it.

Breathing in through all the pores of your body, search out these areas of fatigue. When you find them—for me it is often behind the shoulder blades, but it can be anywhere—open to them and breathe into them. Try to let go of your resistance to these feelings of terrible fatigue and relax into them, surrendering into them fully. You are searching and looking: where does my body feel crushing fatigue? Let the feeling of fatigue—the more overwhelming the better—bleed back into your conscious mind.

This kind of somatic fatigue is not necessarily pleasant. You may find places that feel so weighted and so burdened, so incredibly heavy in an awful way, that you feel you could die. That place in your body may feel like you yourself would feel when you haven't slept for two days. You feel you would like to just drop into the earth and let it all go. It is easy to see why we do not allow that feeling into our conscious reality easily. As you carry on with the practice, you may well find one place after another with this tremendous tiredness. When you do come upon such a place, bring your awareness right to it and try to let yourself slowly melt into it and dissolve into it. This is where the gate to sleep lies, in the heavy, even overwhelming darkness of this somatic fatigue.

The best-case scenario, as you continue with the practice, is that you may find your entire inner Soma relaxing and opening up; the field may be empty, spacious, and free, and at some points you may even feel that you are roaming in a vast, fragrant field of summer grasses and flowers, at night under the starry sky. And then you just drift off into sweet slumber. Although this may sound like an unrealistically romantic rendition, this experience does in fact occur for practitioners, and it is not as uncommon as one might think. As you work with Whole Body Breathing and get to know it better, your body is going to become familiar with the pathway into this delicious territory of sleep.

But, as may more often be the case, let's say you still cannot go back to sleep; it doesn't matter how fully or how deeply you are within your body. Nothing is happening; you can't get back to sleep; it isn't working. In relation to this situation, I am going to make a suggestion that comes from Tibetan yoga, Buddhist retreat experience, and my own years of solitary retreat. Keep going with the Rooting Enhancement: breathe into your cells, reach down into them, and try to feel what they are feeling. Keep going with it until, as will happen eventually, you are really there; awake, not sleeping, but not thinking either. You are resting—not asleep but not diurnally awake either—within the reality of your cells. You may glimpse your cells' awareness as clear and open. At this point, don't be worrying that you are not asleep. It is true you are not asleep, or at least you feel you are not asleep, but you are also not awake in the usual way; you are awake and aware, or your cells are, but your psycho-physical being is actually resting very deeply. You may really surprise yourself to find that, the next morning after not much actual, unconscious sleep at all, you feel fine or maybe, even, you feel wonderfully refreshed and alive.

10

Practice Six:
Twelvefold Lower-Belly Breathing

OVERVIEW

Twelvefold Lower-Belly Breathing is used extensively in all the practicing lineages of Buddhism and also in Hindu yoga. I myself first learned it from my friend Edo Roshi in 1981; a yoga teacher, who was an academic student of mine, showed me some important refinements shortly thereafter. And when I was training in Mahamudra where this same practice is extremely important, it became a staple for me and has remained so ever since.

At this point, it may be helpful for me to share with you how Twelvefold Lower-Belly Breathing is explained in the Tibetan tradition. Beneath the operations of our thinking mind runs our prana, or life force. This energy runs through channels or pathways known as *nadis*. The most important of these is the central channel with which you now have some experience. On either side of the central channel, almost abutting it, are two other principal nadis carrying feminine and masculine energy. These connect with weblike nadi structures in our major energy centers known as *chakras*. All told, there are said to be eighty-four thousand nadis in the body. This representation may sound rather complicated, but it really is needed to clarify the experience we are going to have within the body. I'll be talking about all of this more later on. The conceptualizing that our ego is constantly manufacturing tends to tangle up our nadis and disconnect them from the central channel. What this means experientially is that our conscious experience gets disconnected from the underlying infinitude of our basic being, our unconditional awareness or "natural state." So our prana gets trapped in endless loops, can no longer flow into and through the all-purifying central channel, and therefore becomes stale or polluted. The result is that our experience of life is fundamentally scattered, cloudy, obstructed, and confused. Since we have lost access to our nonconceptual experience, we tend to live in our facsimile versions. Having lost touch with the central channel, we have lost contact with our groundless ground, the natural state, our basic nature, and hence with our true Self and our life.

Twelvefold Lower-Belly Breathing does two things, which are two aspects of the same process. First, through a vigorous out-breath, stale or polluted prana is cleared out of our system. Since stale prana underlies all of our dysfunction, whether physical, energetic, emotional, or spiritual, this emptying-out process is highly beneficial. Then, second, the vigorous out-breath also brings our prana into the central channel. As this happens, our peripheral nadis untangle themselves. As we are about to see, the subjective experience of all of this can be powerful and profound.

The uses and benefits of this practice are many. All of them have to do with coming strongly back into our true body, our Soma. Most importantly, it is a way of bringing ourselves back, when we find ourselves checked out, wildly conceptual, overrun with emotions, frantic, or sunken in depression—that is, when we are one way or another lost in our heady and energetically confused versions of reality.

Coming strongly back to our Soma, our prana enters the central channel. At this point, there can be a very heightened experience of the emptiness of the central channel and of the energetic aspect of the emptiness. Hence, even if we aren't having any particular problem such as those mentioned above, Twelvefold Lower-Belly Breathing is the quickest and most effective way for our awareness to enter and inhabit our empty, open, primordial "core." It is this use that makes it so helpful for any kind of Pure Awareness practice and (to say again) to address physical and emotional ill-health of all kinds. Khenpo Tsultrim Gyamtso, one of my principal Mahamudra teachers, once said that in traditional Tibet, this practice was considered the only medicine and the only doctor you needed with you in long, solitary retreats.

THE PRACTICE

To begin, take the lying-down position that you are now familiar with. We will learn this practice lying down and then later see what it is like to do it in the sitting-up posture. In the various practicing lineages, this practice is mostly done sitting up in order to enhance and further meditation practice. We are going to start with lying down so that we can experience the full range of possibilities that are available in this form of belly breathing.

In the lying-down position, then, just feel the earth under you; then put your awareness completely into your body. Feel that you are extending your consciousness into your body so that you are identified with it. Feel your lower belly and be in there for a few moments. Now pick a spot roughly midway between the perineum and the navel in the lower belly. We are going to begin by breathing into that spot. Visualize that you're breathing in—just do that for a minute or so. As you did with Yin Breathing, bring the breath in, not from the nose through the trachea and down that way, but just directly and immediately into the lower belly on the in-breath, right into that spot. This is all preliminary to the actual Twelvefold Lower-Belly Breathing. Throughout this practice, keep in mind that you are going to be keeping your attention continually within the lower belly; don't let your focus wander afield from that place.

To emphasize: keep your focus continually within the lower belly and don't allow it to rise to your upper abdomen, your heart, or your head. There may be a temptation, particularly if you have some experience with Hindu kundalini, to depart from the instructions and run the energy of the lower belly up the central channel. Please avoid that temptation; you will not only miss the intent and benefit of the practice, but you'll run the risk of seriously damaging yourself physically, energetically, or psychologically.

Now, relaxing your awareness into that spot, take a relatively slow, gentle, medium to full in-breath into the lower belly; no forcing, just what feels comfortable. Next, keeping your attention there, you're going to exhale and attempt to empty out all of the breath, all of the stale prana in the lower belly. This is going to be quite a strong exhale. Do the exhalation slowly; no huffing and puffing, no abrupt forcing. Check with your body to see how much vigor it wants you to apply. How much is enough? How much is too much? If you have a physical condition that suggests you go gently, trust that sense. Some people inherently find too much effort doesn't feel right; again, trust your body's own feeling about it.

What we are looking for here is the sensation of tightening down the lower belly to absolute zero on the out-breath. Imagine you are completely closing it down to nothing. So in-breath is a medium to full in-breath into the lower belly. And then out-breath: empty, empty, empty, empty, and tightening the lower belly down to nothing, emptying out every last cubic millimeter of breath. So now please do one set of twelve breaths. Make sure to take your time; there is no rush; let your body tell you how quickly or slowly to go.

After you have completed this set, just rest quietly and put your awareness once again into your body. Notice the difference. See if there is a kind of still or even vastly peaceful feeling. See if you experience a kind of silvery, energetic flow through the interior space of the body. It's like a lively electricity flowing through the empty, open, body-space, through the entire body: the limbs, torso, head. If you are feeling that, try to be completely with that sensation right now, just be totally with it. Put your awareness into it.

This energy harmonizes and heals our entire somatic state of being, so the more you can identify with it, the better. And this also relaxes the body further. If you have any tight spots, just run that energy through—just bring that silvery electricity through the tight spots and see if you can let go a bit more. Relax.

Now we are going to do a second set of Twelvefold Breathing lying down and I am going to offer you some additional instructions to enhance the practice. At this point, you may find that your lower belly is a bit warm, so we'll be able to go a little further. On the in-breath you can roll the top of your hips forward and puff out your lower belly just a little, and that will lift the lower back off the floor or at least unweight it, very slightly. And on the out-breath, roll the lower back into the floor and pull the pubic bone up and back toward the spine. So you will be developing a slight rolling motion: in-breath, belly puffs out slightly and lower back rolls off the floor; out-breath, belly is pulled back and in and the lower back rolls to the floor. You will need to practice this a little in order to see what I am talking about.

On the out-breath press the lower back into the floor. This rolling motion will help additionally loosen up the strictures in the nadis, the energy pathways in our body, and facilitate the release of the stale, stagnant prana in the lower belly and elsewhere. As you do this next set of twelve breaths, feel that you are filling the lower belly with that delicious in-breath: fresh and cool. And then empty out. How thorough can you make your out-breath? Go ahead and begin your second set of twelve lower-belly breaths.

When you are finished with your second set of Twelvefold

Lower-Belly Breathing, you can just lie quietly and feel what is going on, with the energy flowing in your body throughout the pathways; see if doesn't feel almost like liquid light. Luxuriate in the so-very-tangible, physical quality of the experience.. Notice how steady that energy is. It is independent of everything else in your experience that might be going on right now. You might be having different emotions or feelings as you begin, but notice how this energy is underneath that. You may feel exhausted, but—again—this energy is bright, alive, and completely free of that fatigue. It is running well beneath any relative experience you may be having "higher up."

The energy you are feeling is in fact the "boundary energy" that manifests right on the upper verge of the vast and utter emptiness of our fundamental Soma, our basic nature. The quantum emptiness of our deepest body is constantly giving birth to the energy of our life, and what you are experiencing with Twelvefold Lower-Belly Breathing is the exact place where that empty, infinite space is birthing or translating into that energy; you are feeling that energy in its most primal state. In Tibetan tradition, this is explicitly known as the life force and you are touching it here in it most pure and pristine form.

So just feel that in your body; feel how powerful it is, and how pure. When you die, this energy goes with you. It is part of your fundamental awareness. Unlike the other, more conditioned energy that disappears at death, because it dissolves back into this fundamental energy, your life force in its most primal form is part of "you" for ever and ever. What this energy holds is you—as the you that has always been and always will be—a soul in transformation, a unique presence and beingness, nothing solid or unchanging but always evolving. The basic space of our fundamental nature holds all of our karmic past, present, and future—all of the conditionality that makes up who and what we are—and this energy, as it arises, holds that Totality and offers it forward into our life. At this point, just be with that energy as fully as you can. So the life force in its most primordial form that we are experiencing here is not confined to life—it is more basic and it gives birth to life, as we know it.

This life force, that you are knowing right now in your body, is the very same life force that emerged in the first millisecond of the life of the universe. And it is right here, in the body, that we humans not only have contact with that primordial power but are able to realize that we ourselves arise from it moment by moment, as does everything else that is.

Here, then, we are starting to tap into the source of Being itself. How do you feel about this right now? What do you think about it? It gives much food for thought, does it not? This is where being comes from, where life comes from, and where our personal existence comes from; when you learn to be in touch with this level of your own being, there's a continual healing and purifying quality to our entire state of being and our experience of our lives. In this practice, we're allowing the purity of life that arises to permeate us; then we are less vulnerable to getting caught by our own karmic patterns, our activation, our habitual pain, hunger, and confusion, and so on. It is such a simple practice but with such profound impacts; it is pretty amazing.

PART THREE

How the Practices Unfold

11

Intention, Attention, Sensation, and Discipline

Through the six core practices of Somatic Meditation, a very fundamental reorientation occurs in our relationship to our body; in fact, a radical transformation comes about. At the beginning, we may be so absorbed in the self-enclosed circuitry of our left brain that we have little or no cognizance of our Soma at all; or we perceive it dimly through a haze of mental projections, judgments, and interpretations. In this case, we have little or no direct contact with our actual body and are experiencing mainly a set of mental projections that we take to be our body.

Through the somatic practices we eventually end up in a very different place. Now we are able to be fully present within our nonconceptual—which means our actual—body and to experience it with absolute simplicity and directness. We—our conscious self—are now in dialogue with that body; we are able to understand its language, respect what it knows, and, most importantly, from a practical standpoint, follow its directives.

In order to illustrate the journey of our "radicalization" in relation to our Soma, I am going to outline six principal phases, levels,

or steps that we go through in working with each of the six protocols. In order to provide you with a concrete sense of what the
somatic protocols actually are and some understanding of how
they unfold through the six phases, I will be using the Ten Points
practice as an example. As you read this description, though, keep
in mind that each of the other somatic protocols also evolves
through these same six steps or phases, although each does so in a
somewhat different and characteristic way.

Although I am going to talk about six phases as if they were
distinct stages, in fact they lead naturally one into the other; thus,
in practice, the journey here occurs in one, unbroken, seamless
unfolding. I am artificially talking about discrete steps so that you
can have some conceptual understanding of what the journey of
each protocol is and how it works. It is perhaps similar to a river
that runs on and on, in one continuous, unbroken flow; and yet,
to orient ourselves, we might put markers up on the bank at each
mile, so as we travel the river we can say, "Okay, now we are at one
mile, two miles," and so forth. But the internal process of the river
doesn't have those markers at all.

Please also keep in mind that in this section we are going to
be creating a conceptual framework for something that is really
only fully known nonconceptually. It is important that we don't
confuse what we understand conceptually with the actual experience of the process, which is ever so much more rich, subtle,
multifaceted, interesting, informative—and unexpected—than any
abstracted version could ever be. This will be a long discussion so
I will break it up into several chapters.

1. Intention

The first step in developing a new and more direct relationship
with our Soma is forming an appropriate and functional intention. At first glance, this may seem like an obvious and easily
understandable point, but there is a lot here. Whatever we direct

our intention to, we pay attention to; and whatever we pay attention to, neurologically, becomes the direction in which we grow and develop awareness. If our intention is to try to allay our anxiety through eating chocolate cake, then we will move in that direction and we will strengthen the neurological pathways that associate relief of anxiety with eating chocolate cake. If our intention, on the other hand, is to meet our problem of increased anxiety with somatic exploration, we might defer the chocolate cake solution "just for now" and go do some body work to get inside ourselves and try to see what's really going on. Then, equally or far more so, we might find relief from our anxiety. Just as the initial intentions were quite different, so are the outcomes.

So our first step is to set our intention toward our body: "I prioritize my body and my relationship to it." This needs to be a real intention based on an understanding of why this is essential for us right now. And thus even to form a strong and functional intention, there needs to be a coherent and clear comprehension of the overall path to spiritual embodiment and the critical place of the somatic-practices work within it.

2. Directed Attention

Initially, most of us do not have a very clear or positive intention toward our body. In fact, to start with, we are so habituated to trying to live in our conceptual mind that we may not even be aware of an issue here at all. The result is an unconscious, negative relationship to our Soma. Let's say our life revolves around a hectic lifestyle, being "busy" all the time, working, shopping, relating to our domestic life, including many hours spent on the Internet, watching TV, and reading and writing e-mails—all largely left-brain activities—running through our ever expanding "to do " list, "accomplishing things," entertaining ourselves, seeing friends, and accumulating more and more information.

Here, the unconscious, negative intention toward our body

comes out in paying less and less attention to the domain of the Soma and perhaps not even noticing it, as what little awareness we have of it slips further and further away; we are more and more losing touch with the feeling of our physicality, our corporeal beingness, our sense experience, our feelings, the hum of our parasympathetic organism within, the imaginal life that lies behind and beneath our thinking, and the roots of our emotional life in our limbic system. We are drying up inside; we are fast on the road to becoming a desiccated husk of a human; and of course, we are part of a larger, global campaign, with our increasingly shared world culture becoming a desiccated husk of a society and a desiccated husk of a world. In turning toward our left brain with so much attention and avidity, so much energy and ambition, we are turning away, minute by minute, hour by hour, day by day, from our Soma, our true Self, and our true life—and Life itself. As mentioned, when we don't pay attention to something, our capacity to experience it diminishes and, then, over time, atrophies. In this case, the neural pathways that link our somatic experience with our left-brain thinking mind begin to become nonfunctional and die off. Then, increasingly, we lose the capacity to feel or sense our body even at a rudimentary level.

Step two in recovering our body is to *pay attention* to our Soma. Using Ten Points as our example, then, beginning with the toes, we systematically work our way up through the body, breathing in through our pores, attending to each area in detail, to begin the process of resuscitation and reconnection. In Ten Points, we are working mostly with the more surface layers of our somatic experience. The subtler internal explorations come with later protocols.

When we arrive at the first instruction, "pay attention to your big toe on each foot," at first, practitioners may not be able to do this because, they often report, they have no feeling not only of their toes, but often of their feet, their legs, or even the lower half of their body. They can't pay attention because they don't have anything to pay attention to. "Keep trying," I tell them. For even directing our attention to the vicinity of where we think the toes should or might be is already transforming our neurological wiring. If we keep at it, pretty soon we begin to be able to locate our toes, not in terms of our mental image of where we think they are, but from the inside, exactly what they feel like, where they actually are, where they live, so to speak. And so with the rest of the body, the toes on upward, the front part of the foot right behind the toes, the ball of the feet, the instep, the outside of the feet, the arch, the sole, the anklebones on the inside and outside, the ankle, and so on upward. In the beginning, you work with one area, then the next, then the next. When you first practice Ten Points, you work on each part, big toes, second toes, and so on and upward. As you move from one part of your body to the next, you forget about the parts you have already worked on. You just focus 100 percent on the part you are currently attending to.

However, as you become more familiar with Ten Points, as you move upward through your body, you can continue to include and remain consciously connected with the parts you have already "woken up." So you focus first on your big toes, but then as you move your focus to your second toe, you retain some subliminal somatic awareness of your big toes. As you move your focus to your middle toe, again, you retain some awareness of your big toe and your second toe. Thus when you move to a new area, you do not entirely abandon or leave behind the somatic awareness of what you have already been developing. Similarly, when you are focusing on your knees, for example, you are including in your background somatic awareness everything you have already worked on: your feet, your ankles, and your lower legs. By the time you get to your head and are focusing on your face, you are retaining some background somatic awareness of the entire rest of your body.

So it is that in your practice, as you move up through the body, Ten Points becomes more and more inclusive of the whole sum.

In the somatic practices in general then, you first learn them piecemeal and then it will be quite natural for you to work with them in ever more integrated patterns. In this, you are beginning to develop new capacities and dimensions of awareness; now awareness is beginning to become no longer exclusive or even local. As we make this journey, we will see for ourselves that our awareness operates in more and more holistic ways. We thought it was elsewise for no other reason than because we *thought* it was elsewise.

3. Noticing and Feeling Sensation

As we pay attention to the various parts of our body in Ten Points, initially we may simply feel that they are numb or even dead. This, in itself, is a welcome development, because these feelings of numbness or deadness are important feelings; we know directly—not through our incessantly thinking and interpreting left brain—what is going on there. Even in the feeling of numbness or deadness, our body is beginning to wake up; our capacity is developing.

As we continue the practice, the felt-sense of our body, the feelings and sensations, become more differentiated, subtle, and clear. In attending to our big toes, we may next feel some kind of density, massiveness, or unpleasant heaviness. Subsequently, painful feelings may appear—a dull achiness, twinges of pain, or tiny, unpleasant micro-spasms. Further along still, we find we can feel the surging life of the big toe, the flow and pulse of blood and lymph, the tingling of neurological sensation, the inner density of the bone, the thickness of surrounding fascia and flesh, even the brittleness of the toenail, the temperature on our skin, the pressure, perhaps, of socks and the floor beneath. And while we can mentally classify each sensation into some logical group— say, "skin" or "blood and lymph flow"—in fact the more we do the practice the more it dawns on us that each moment of experience of the big toe is its own thing; in some real sense it is fresh and unique. Labeling each sensation is irrelevant and actually gets between us and what we are feeling; at a certain point, we no longer feel the need—if I may coin a verb—to "left-brain" what is happening. For, as we say in our lineage, the Soma never repeats itself.

We come to the strong suspicion that even within our big toe, there is a vast, perhaps limitless universe of possible things to discover. Amazingly, already we are beginning to make contact with the actual somatic reality of our big toe, outside and independent of our logical, categorizing mind and its frameworks. The Soma's own interior landscape, its awareness and knowledge of itself, are coming on-line, and we are connecting with it. As with the big toe, so with each other part of the body we explore. Each has its own kind of preexisting awareness, its own domain of experience, its own vistas to uncover and receive, all of which it is glad to tell us about. Not just glad, either, for the mission of each sensation, each moment of somatic experience, is to communicate itself to our conscious mind and thus fulfill its mission for being. As mentioned, Ten Points can be done every day for years and, so it seems, we never run out of new and deeply compelling worlds to explore, worlds that change us literally from the ground up.

4. Discipline: Returning When Attention Wanders Away

Initially, we are following the live or recorded (or written) guidance of an experienced teacher and finding ourself in a rapidly unfolding process of new discovery and empowerment. We may feel much inspiration, especially when we notice the opening, the nourishment, the healing, and the increasingly somatic presence that the instruction is making possible for us. As we become more familiar with the practices, with each practice we come to a point when we have understood it well enough and have sufficiently incorporated its format, so that we are becoming able to do it without external guidance.

As we are poised to go further and deeper, particularly when we are practicing on our own, we run into a serious problem. We find that sometimes or most of the time we are having the hardest time keeping our attention on the practice at hand, staying with the part of the body we are working with, and carrying the protocol beyond a certain point. We keep being pulled off by our discursive thinking. Many times, we exit into thinking about some current situation or event in our life. Ironically, so it seems, sometimes we separate from our body as a result of the increased sensitivity and openness developed in practice itself: we are so taken by some new somatic discovery that we cannot resist thinking about it: "Wow! This is amazing."

But the moment we think about it, of course we have lost it and are no longer within the Soma. First, we feel we are really there, within our body; the next moment, without noticing it, we have popped up to our head and are off thinking about something. Our mind feels quite unsteady and unstable; distressingly, we seem to have very little control over it or ability to stay with the practice. This kind of recognition of how little actual control we have over our mental process can be not only perplexing but also anxiety producing. "What's going on? Am I doing the practice wrong? Am I regressing? Or am I perhaps just incapable?"

In fact, this is a normal and natural development. All along our mind has been that unsteady and unstable, that prone to be taken over by discursive thinking. We just haven't seen it until now because we were too taken with and taken over by our thinking, too enamored and mesmerized by it. Even when first doing the somatic work, perhaps we were so entranced with the novelty and intensity of the practice that there wasn't room for information to come through about the extent and strength of our discursive tendency. Again, maybe we have been somewhat aware of it but now, deeply inspired by the journey we have embarked upon, our attachment to thinking is hitting us freshly in the face and is felt now to be much more distressing.

Now the gritty work begins. When the mind wanders away from the body work, just bring it back. One needs to be patient and steady: every time we find ourself having abandoned the Soma and having drifted away into some discursive fantasy, simply, gently, but without hesitation, rancor, or negotiation, bring it back.

The process of bringing the mind back again and again accomplishes some important things. First, when the mind wanders off, it is looking for some wishful-thinking, fantasized gratification, some imaginary "payoff," that being within the simple "isness" of the Soma does not provide. This is a neurotic, addictive tendency; by short-circuiting that tendency in mid-course by bringing our attention back to the body, before it gets very far, we are undermining it. Once we stop driving in this neurotic, ultimately self-defeating neurological rut in the open fields of our mind, the grass of fresh, living experience can begin to grow back.

Second, by bringing the mind back again and again, we develop the habit of returning to the Soma; we are building a new and different pathway through the spacious field, one much more in keeping with respect for the habitat: namely, our own person, the totality of our living experience, and our journey. And third, over time, we begin to find a kind of corporeal relief and satisfaction, and relaxation, which discursive thinking is quite incapable of providing. This becomes a repeated and repeatable experience, and it tends to help us remain within the integrity of our body and the practice.

1 2

Tension and Breathing

L et us continue to use Ten Points practice as a representative example of how the six steps function with each of the protocols of the "body work." Now we are going to look at step 5.

5. Working with Tension

NOTICING TENSION

As we continue, we enter more fully into contact with our big toe; our experience of it becomes more refined, and we are able to return to it more frequently and stay close to it better. At this point, we begin to notice something else.

As we saw in our practice, there seems to be quite a bit of tension in our big toe. Initially, we might feel this as a mass of tightness where the big toe joins with the foot. It is as if, right where the toe meets the body of the foot, there is a bunching up of overly restricted, dense fascia. The more we feel into it, the more we may experience it as quite unpleasant. Further investigation reveals additional, subtler tension along the sides of the big toe, then on the bottom, in the mass of the big toe itself, in the toenail and, as we become more sensitive and discerning, in the bone of the toe. The amount of sensation in the toe bone is surprising, and it reflects the very high level of metabolic activity in the bones, known to be surpassed only by that of the brain and the liver.

As we move to the other toes, then on through the various other parts of the foot, the fascia, the fluids, and the bones, we similarly notice the presence of tension. And this tension continues to enter our awareness as we carry out Ten Points practice throughout our entire body. In each place, as our ability to sense becomes more refined, the more we notice tension. How might this tension be experienced? In addition to what feels like the natural, unaffected being of each part of our body, we sense some kind of quite unpleasant overlay. Something seems to be leaning on, impinging upon, or restricting our otherwise free, open, and easy sensation of that part; some vague sense of artificial gripping or holding on seems to be happening there. We might have a subtle feeling of wanting to get rid of it so that we can "liberate" that part.

When we first experience tension, it seems to be an essentially localized phenomenon. For example, when we are working with a particular part of our body, we may initially notice tension in one area of that part but not notice it elsewhere. With our big toe, initially we might have felt that the tension really lies at the juncture of big toe and foot. But then the more we look into it, the more we find that, no, it is also on the sides, in the mass, in the toenail and bone, and so on—it is more general, not as strictly localized, as we may have first thought.

With each part of our body, we are first going to notice the more extensive, tightest, or most obvious tension; then we see that the tightness and restriction lie in other, adjacent areas of that part, too. With the big toe and the other locales of our body we are exploring, eventually we begin to suspect that tension seems to completely pervade the entire locale, though at various levels, like the successive layers of a many-layered cake: there is the gross tension on the surface; then less obvious, subtler levels of tension beneath; then, finally, the subtlest and most refined tension at the deepest layers.

We may even have the subtle bodily intuition that the tension is actually present all the way down to the cellular level and that quite possibly each of the cells of our body is tense. As noted, the biological sciences tell us that, in fact, this is so; one can talk about the cellular dysfunction or tension, restricting oxidation, nourishment, and neurological functioning of our cells. And so it seems not altogether impossible that it is ultimately this cellular tension that we are sensing as we carry out the Ten Points practice and that appears at more noticeable and grosser levels as it approaches the threshold of our clear conscious awareness.

UNDERSTANDING TENSION

How may we understand this tension, where it comes from, and how we might work with it? As our practice continues, as already suggested, we begin to sense some subtle connection between the tension in our body and our tendency to exit from our experience into the isolation and disconnection of left-brain thinking. Now we can explore this process of disconnection in more detail.

When something occurs that we do not want to see or feel, we have a strong tendency to freeze and exit into thinking. It could be an internal or an external event. Perhaps a memory suddenly pops up of a painful interaction we had yesterday. In the instant of the memory abruptly appearing, we have a feeling of some kind of vague *something* in our body, in the Soma's simple and nonjudgmental way of knowing. The initial experience is neutral, but it *is* some kind of eventfulness, some kind of energy and, as with any new event, we fear it. In a split second, we freeze, we tense up, and exit; we separate, label it, and attribute a definite source to it, to what happened yesterday. We are trying to get our familiar ground back. We begin to think about it, trying to "work it out," attaching all kinds of judgments, interpretations, and perhaps strategies to it, setting it within the constantly running ego narrative, the map, of who we think we are or are trying to be. In that split second between the naked experience and finding ourselves gone into our left brain, something very important has occurred. We turned away from the raw, somatic reality of the visceral felt sense toward a disconnected, mental—and much less viscerally painful—version of it. A disembodied, abstract version. The map of our conceptualized "me."

Through the somatic protocols, we begin to be able to track this process in an ever increasingly precise way. We begin to become aware of how we accomplish turning away from the open and unmediated experience of our body; we do that by literally hardening our body so that we no longer feel. Something painful or even just slightly unpleasant happens and two things occur simultaneously—in fact, they are part of one process: we tense our body and we jump into our thinking mind. Hardening our body so that we no longer feel the painful thing is part and parcel of exiting into thinking; exiting into thinking is inseparable from hardening our body even further against the feeling. We tense up, and it *is* "up"; rightly, we never say "tense down." But we do say "calm down," which is exactly accurate to the process of releasing tension and returning to our Soma.

GETTING INSIDE TENSION, TAKING OWNERSHIP, AND RELEASING

When people first develop the ability to sense the life in their big toe, when you ask them if they can feel any tension there, they may reply "no." And so with the other areas of their body: initially they may have little or no knowledge of any particular tension or of being tense at all. This reflects the fact that not only is tension the primary somatic mechanism of repression of experience, but even knowledge of becoming tense itself is often unconscious. Perhaps we have some subliminal fear that even to acknowledge tension itself would be to open a whole can of worms. At the same time, once people are invited to explore their big toe (for example) for signs of tension, eventually they drop to a new level of somatic awareness. They enter into a whole series of discoveries of the major places of tension in their bodies; now, it literally seems to be everywhere.

However, this awareness is still too external; we are viewing the tension from the outside, as alien and other. At this point, I will instruct people to try to put their awareness *inside* their tension. "What would it be like to experience your tension, in this or that place, not just from the outside, but from within itself?" This may seem implausible to them and even impossible at first, but as so often in the body work, the impossible turns out to be eminently doable and, eventually, completely obvious. You have perhaps seen this in the protocols we have just carried out.

The practice is to bring your awareness right to your tension—say, at the junction of big toe and foot—and then try to surrender your awareness into the tension there. This may sound like a fairly advanced practice, because, after all, you are being asked to give up the dualistic standpoint of self and other—here your big-toe tension—and dissolve your awareness into the other. But the body is a wonderful—in fact the premier and perhaps only true—access point to moments of a truly nondual and authentically self-aware state of being. The body is quite capable of experiencing itself, without the intervention of dualistic consciousness.

Once we find ourselves inside our tension, if even for just a moment, a few very interesting things happen that foreshadow later, clearer experiences on the path. First, in that moment of "being inside," we cannot tell if it is still "we" who are aware or whether it is really just the body being aware of itself. There is no conclusion to be drawn here particularly, but it does open up a field of uncertainty about who we are and what the body is that is extremely interesting.

Once "inside," we also no longer see the tension as something *other* that has happened *to* us. In fact, we can feel in it a "me," a subtle ego consciousness, that is hanging on, maintaining the tension, refusing for its—our—own purposes to let go and relax. This discovery represents a hugely important moment: by entering the tension, *we have pushed back the boundary of the unconscious and can now see the previously unconscious ego agency maintaining the tension.*

As long as we did not realize that it was "we" who were tensing and holding on, we were unable to take any responsibility for it; we were unable to own it and gain agency in relation to it. By putting the agency on the "other," the body, we were in a state of disempowerment. But, in realizing and feeling, quite clearly, that it is indeed "we" who are holding on, we have taken responsibility for our tensing; and we have gained the capacity to begin to release it. Now the instruction can be given, "inhabit the tension, feel it, and begin to release and let go." Inside the tension, you see exactly how to do this. If you are holding a ball in your hand and you want to drop it, you are aware of your hard gripping and you can just let go. With our somatic awareness of our tension from the inside, it is that simple.

IS TENSION THE SAME AS POLLUTION?

The further instruction is given of what to do with this tension: "release it down into the earth." The natural, unspoken tendency when we let go and relax is to surrender downward, dying— surrendering back into the earth not just surrendering our tension but our entire selves.

Sometimes when I am teaching the body work, there are objections to releasing tension downward. Even though one could respond that this is what the body does in its own natural and unself-conscious operation, more can be said that may be helpful. So the objection is "This doesn't feel right—it feels completely wrong to do that, because I don't want to release my pollution down into the earth; she already has too many problems, too much poisoning." In other words, we can't do what might be the easiest and most natural thing because we judge it as "bad." This is an important moment because something basic to the Western and now the modern mentality is surfacing: a basic distrust of the body, an idea that what it may want, what may seem most natural, is hurtful. This is also a distrust of the capacity of the earth, of nature, to hold the human; these are based, I suspect, on a fundamental mistrust of the human person, his or her process of life, and the whole of nature.

At this moment, I will say to the practitioners as already suggested: your tension is not something fundamentally impure or evil. It is not like pollution. Tension is basic energy; it is the life force; that life force originally came from the earth via the lower belly, the source, and gave birth to everything we are; and it continues to flow into us moment by moment to nourish us and give us life. But in tension, we are misusing the life force that always ultimately belongs to the earth; we are, in a way, damming it up, possessing it for our own, and trying to have it serve our need to fuel the apparent existence of an isolated ego. When we release tension, we are simply returning the dammed-up energy of life to its original status as the primal life force; at that point, it needs and wants to flow back to the earth where it came from and where it is supposed to return, apart from the intervention and disruption of our egoic exploitation. As mentioned, releasing tension back into the earth is the ultimately responsible ecological action, the ultimate recycling.[1]

In the beginning, this teaching may not be readily received, partly because it is not yet experiential for people and partly because it calls into question the fundamental ideology of the evil of the (modern) human and the fallibility of nature, an ideology with deep roots in our Western cultural past. It is not that easy to give up such basic beliefs. But, over time, especially when people are willing to allow themselves the experience of connecting with tension, inhabiting it, and releasing it, their point of view changes. In other words, the experience of the Soma wins out over the ideology of the thinking mind. People see for themselves how wholesome and healthy this kind of release feels, and they see the wonderful physical, psychological, and spiritual gains that come through it. And just at the exact moment of release, they may hear a peal of thunder, the sweep of the wind down the mountains, the cry of a red-tailed hawk, or some other joyful song of the world. What can one possibly say then? At that point, they generally give in; they see they are not really getting much traction out of their previously held negativity. It is clear their body does not go for it and neither does the world.

As I have suggested, the tension we are talking about here isn't experienced only as gross physical, muscular discomfort. We can experience the very same kind of tightening, tensing, and hardening in bones and fascia; in the inner life of our ever-flowing lymph, blood, and breathing; within the energetic feel of our organs; in our emotions; in the pure energy of our inner body; and even in our consciousness. In each of these domains, tension indicates we are resisting and moving away from the nameless threat presented by our naked experience into thinking and judging, into our ego isolation and, ultimately, desolation.

So it is that this practice of releasing tension doesn't apply only to what we might think of as "the body," even in all this multi-dimensionality. In speaking of this process of release, Dogen, the thirteenth-century founder of the Soto lineage of Zen Buddhism in Japan, says, "Let the mind and the body fall away." By "body" he means here the tensed-up, conceptualized body we have been speaking of, the body we assume ourselves to have; by mind, he means the tensed up, reactive emotional/mental process of separating and retreating into mental disconnection. You let both fall away and what remains is the naked Soma, present to itself, aware of itself. This is the moment of realization for Dogen and for us.

We could say that through stage five we are gaining the capacity to feel our tension and then to release it; it is where we are learning the specific tools and techniques of working with tensing and letting go. As with other stages, this is a process: we need to be instructed in the details of the practice, one by one, then we need to rehearse those details, internalize them, then reap their rewards, understand them, and incorporate them into our state of being. This takes time because, as always, we need to do enough of the practice to gain familiarity and neurological capacity. We need to put some miles on the tires. But in time, this just becomes who we are; in time, we integrate stage five into our way and feeling of being human, into our body. At that point, in our meditation we can simply come to our body with its tensions and—drawing on all the learning and all the capacity we have developed—just relax into the "immeasurable expanse" of what is.

Contemporary Dzogchen teachers, fully in alignment with Dogen's famous saying, often portray realization as a somatic process in just this way. To let go of the ego, we have to completely relax; the more we completely relax, the less ground ego has and it begins to become less solid; it begins to dissolve. To let go of the ego, let go of all the somatic tension. The same teaching is found in early Buddhism where we read, "In reference to the seen, there will be only the seen. In reference to the heard, only the heard. In reference to the sensed, only the sensed. In reference to the cognized, only the cognized."[2] All of these teachings refer to the pure experience of the body—that is, somatic experience, with no overlay, no freezing, no tension. Again, the teachings of Dzogchen: relaxation is the key to enlightenment. These are all essentially equivalent ways of saying that the release of tension is the somatic way of talking about the letting go of ego; and it shows the somatic gate as the core of this process. It is the key moment on the path; it is a glimpse of realization.

6. Breathing Practice

As we have already seen in the previous discussion and in its guided meditations, the somatic practices develop awareness by drawing on two basic techniques. The first is attention. When we direct our attention to some place in our body, this brings awareness to that place; and that place begins to wake up; we begin to be aware of it either for the first time or in newer, subtler ways. We begin to have a new experience of it.

The second way the practices develop awareness is through the breath. In many of the somatic practices, we use the breath as a vehicle for and an enhancement of our attention and our awareness. The breath, as used in the somatic protocols, has three progressively more refined dimensions. First is the *outer breath,* which is our physical breathing in of the air around us. Second is the *inner breath*—the prana (India), *lung* (Tibet), or qi (China)— which is, at a subtler level, the vitalizing energy lying beneath and within the outer breath, of which the outer breath is a more concrete physical expression (we have also called this, in its most elemental form, "the life force"). Third is the *secret breath,* the quantum emptiness that is the core or essence of the inner breath; this is unconditioned awareness itself which, as already suggested, gives birth to the inner breath. These are all dimensions of the breath because when you fathom the physical breath you discover the energetic breath and when you fathom the energetic breath to its essence you discover the secret breath.

We can practice, then, feeling the outer breath enter not only through our respiratory system but also through all the pores of our body. In addition, we can simply visualize breathing our breath—and now it is the inner breath, the life force—entering into interior spaces. Strangely, as we saw above, we can also sometimes physically feel the inner breath entering into interior places in our body, such as directly into the lower belly. Or, in some of the more advanced practices, we trace back to the secret breath to enter and touch—within our body—the limitless awareness that is the source, the ground and most basic nature, of our breath and of our entire somatic being.

Whenever you are working with the breath, even at a very beginning level, all three of these dimensions are present. In the early stages of practice, you may only be aware of the outer breath, but as your practice matures, you will gradually sense the deeper and subtler layers of your breathing. Similarly, in the early stages of Somatic Meditation, attention and breath—and the awareness they lead to—seem like distinct realities that need to be practiced as separate items. Later, though, you will realize that attention, breath, and awareness are actually one thing: when you attend, you bring breath to that place; breathing to a certain place brings the life force and the awareness to that place. Whether you know it or not, you are always working with the totality of what the breath is.

Within the protocols, there are many ways in which the breath is used. At the simplest level, it provides a vehicle on which our intention and attention can ride. We can visualize ourselves breathing into our big toe, in through all its pores and directly into its interior. This bringing in of the outer breath, then feeling the inner breath or life force within it, and finally experiencing the awareness that the life force carries as its core all greatly enhance and strengthen our Ten Points practice with our big toe: our attention is more focused, simple, and pure, and the experience of the big toe can become subtler, more nuanced, and more profound. In Ten Points practice, in particular, the breath enables a much higher degree of experiential vividness and differentiation as we move from the big toes on through the entire rest of the body.

The breath also helps us explore the inner spaces of the body in a way that enhances our practice significantly. Within the body, as we have seen, there are many interior vortices where an experience of radical openness and emptiness can be found; and where, as we shall presently see, we will find our own most fundamental openness, emptiness, and freedom. These include (among many others) the perineum, the sexual center in the lowest regions of the lower belly, the hara or lower dan t'ien, the navel, the solar plexus, the base of the throat, the throat, the back of the palate, the middle of the skull, the top of the skull, and (of particular importance for meditation, as we have already seen) the central channel. By breathing directly into these places or in some cases simply following the natural flow of the breath there, we are able to connect with the basic space and unique energetic aspect available in each; each functions, then, as a "gate" to the primordial state, and the breath enables us to come to the entrance to, and later to step through, each of these gates.

At a more advanced level, the breath is used to connect us with the subtle energy of our own internal being. Beneath and undergirding our "physical" body is what is called the subtle body, an underlying aspect of our being that is experienced as highly refined, thoroughly fluid energy that colors and enlivens the open, empty field of our basic Soma or ultimate nature. As we become more experienced practitioners, we are able to use the breath to connect with the energy that defines our subtle body. For example, we may breathe into the central channel and after a while begin to feel a subtle up-flow. This is the body's own inner, subtle breath, apart from any "practice" we may be doing. We have perhaps already had a glimpse of this up-flow in the previous practice section with the Central Channel guided meditation. We realize that up-flow was already there, and in fact is going on all the time there; by "breathing" into the central channel, we are able to realize that, to discover, connect with, and align ourselves with it. These examples only begin to suggest something of the vast range of opportunities and possibilities in practice with the breath.

In the case of the breath, as with each of the other steps discussed in this section, there can obviously be no question in the initial stages of our practice of fully exploring the territory available or achieving everything that is possible for us there. In the beginning, we are mainly concerned with learning the basic mechanics and aspects of each practice and gaining some initial experience of how it goes. We will be working with the breath and the other aspects of the practices to ever deeper and subtler levels throughout the rest of the journey. But at this stage of our practice, we are laying the foundation for everything on the journey that is going to come later.

1 3

As the Practice Matures

The idea of six protocols and the six aspects to each as I have described them may seem a bit complex and abstract. In order for all of this to come down to earth and feel real, we will need to gain experience. When we first learn the practices of Somatic Meditation, we need to train in the various protocols and see for ourselves how their unfolding occurs. Even if, in the beginning, the schema I am presenting seems a little vague and intangible, there needs to be a commitment to going through things in a deliberate and systematic way without too much concern for making sense of it all. Through this process, the different protocols and the way they mature in our experience will become more and more clear and even obvious.

In addition, in our training, it is important not to rush. For example, in doing Ten Points, because it is the first major somatic protocol, it can be very valuable, as mentioned, to work one's way slowly through the various steps, at least up to one's capacity at that time, perhaps taking several sessions for each. It is helpful to allow ample time to feel into the practice thoroughly and develop your own experience of it. You might stay with each step long enough for it to feel somewhat assimilated and integrated and in place. Then you go on to the next step and so on, doing the same thing with the other protocols. Remember, the whole spiritual journey is about coming into our own embodiment more fully and completely, so the more time we take in the beginning, the more solidly we lay the foundation for what comes later and the more accessible and easily learned subsequent practices will be.

Just to reiterate, the reason for taking time with each protocol and its stages is to grow and develop the neural pathways in that area. With Ten Points, for example, you find the more you do it the more you are able to do it. You are developing neurological capacity. Though you may be taught the practice, going through all the stages, in the beginning you may only have a faint experience of what, later on, you will find very simple, natural, and straightforward—and very much more profound.

While the practices and steps as I am describing them may possibly *sound* a bit tedious, the actual experience isn't like that at all. We train in one protocol, then the second, following the instructions, and the process unfolds in a natural and spacious and generally quite fulfilling way. One thing leads to the next as we follow the thread of our experience; we are assimilating the lessons into our way of being and gaining a feeling of groundedness, simplicity, and ease. As we become more familiar with the protocols and how they go, those practices begin to become second nature; we are able to do them directly and intuitively, without having to think about it. And, strangely enough, this feeling of simplicity, groundedness, and ease begins to permeate our larger life, almost without our realizing it.

The first "movement" in the symphony of our journey, then, is training fully in the somatic protocols, learning the structure of each practice and its various aspects, and assimilating it thoroughly. In so doing, we come to see what the practice is for and what it can accomplish for us. Through this, the journey each protocol embodies becomes part of our system, our process, and our life.

The second movement of our symphony involves practice, practice, and more practice of each protocol. However, in this movement, rather than focusing on mastering and integrating the practice, we are now exploring what happens within it; we are allowing the "container" of the practice to hold us in a safe and familiar environment, while we explore the ever-new experience and ever-fresh discoveries that arise with in.

Much later in our symphony—perhaps it is even the coda—we are able add a free-form element to our practice. It is not that we stop carrying out the practice as taught or stop exploring what happens when we are securely within its protective container; that continues, of course.

But after we have trained for quite some time, our subjective experience might be like this: we feel called to a certain locale in our body (it could literally be anywhere); we sense a restriction in our experience there; based on our past practice, we are now able to feel the restriction as unacceptably uncomfortable; we see directly that we need to meet that restriction, release it downward, opening that space; and we know in a direct, nonconceptual way how to do it. At this point, we don't have to be consciously selecting one of the protocols or running through the six phases deliberately and self-consciously. Working with our body in this way has simply become our natural and preferred way to relate with our experience. This is quite a change from how it was for us earlier on.

Once we have fully trained in the six protocols, then, while we may have a general, conceptual understanding of the protocols and how they unfold, the step that we need to take right at this moment can only be discovered by listening to what the Soma is sending our way, just now. It is the experience of looking into the shadows, not being distracted or sidetracked by our own preconceptions, and waiting until we see the next step, as it is called for by the Soma. And then we need to be willing to trust it and go, "leap to the situation," as Trungpa Rinpoche used to say.

The somatic maturation that occurs in the course of the six steps is a kind of overall process as we learn and practice the various somatic protocols. Different people find some protocols more accessible than others, or more helpful, and will gravitate toward those; different protocols will be particularly needing emphasis of now one, now another of the stages; again, this varies according to the individual practitioner and the place one is in one's training and one's path. This suggests something important: the journey as it unfolds in each of us is not something that can be categorized, objectified, pinned down, generalized, or even anticipated beyond a certain point. This is because it emerges moment by moment out of the darkness of our unique Soma.

Obviously (and to reiterate), in the beginning stages of Somatic Meditation, there can be no question of exploring all the possibilities of the practice or attaining everything that the practice ultimately offers. At this point, we are learning the basic mechanics of the practices, seeing how to be in our body and work with them directly, and gaining some initial experience of how it goes. For example, we will continue to explore the dynamics of sensation, tension, the breath, and release to deeper and subtler levels throughout our entire journey toward the realization of complete embodiment.

In this section, I have been leaning on the more challenging aspects of the somatic journey. At the same time, I want to say, when practitioners take up the body work, their experience is also, and really far more prominently, one of immense relief. They finally have a way to connect with themselves and who they really are; they are given a practical and effective way to relax, release, and let go of huge psychological and mental burdens they may have been carrying; they begin to discover possibilities for themselves and their lives that may never have previously occurred to them; and often they feel that they have come home, found their true place for the first time, not just in themselves, but in the world. And, as mentioned, there is generally a great opening: their inner life and their inner experience are likely to free up unpredictably—sometimes, it seems, beyond all bounds. It is an amazing process for me as a teacher to witness. I never know what is going to happen. But one thing I can be fairly sure of: there will be life-bringing changes on all sorts of levels.

As we bring awareness to our tension, inhabit it, and begin to release it, a new process is set in motion. As we have seen, the tension or restriction has been stubbornly maintaining and reinforcing our rejection and repression of unwelcome experience. Tension has been our way of keeping unwanted thoughts, feelings, memories, images, sensations, emotions, and the like out of sight, buried in our body, in our unconscious. What happens when we start letting go of this repressive mechanism and soften the boundary between the Soma and our consciousness? Now everything that we have been artificially excluding from our everyday awareness is free to come knocking at the door.

What kinds of things come up? When we as practitioners dissolve layers of tension, we typically find that our experience of ourselves opens up quickly and sometimes quite dramatically. Again, what's happening is that previously unconscious material is now flowing up from the Soma. We may come into contact with inspiration and with creative aspects of ourselves we never have felt quite this strongly or clearly before. We may experience feelings of sensitivity, tenderness, appreciation, or love that are new. Visions, dream images, sudden memories, inner pictures—all begin to arise from the Soma in a new way. And, just now, we are only at the very beginning of the somatic journey.

At the same time, we will run into unconscious aspects, our "shadow" material, that call into question and disconfirm our ego versions of ourselves and others. We may now find ourselves noticing a great deal more about our relationships with family members and close friends, becoming aware of how we have been invested in restricted, self-serving versions of people in our life, whether stubbornly and artificially negative or blindly positive; and realizing that there is much more to those people than we have been willing to see. Having perhaps had the impression that the responsibility for troubled relationships lay mainly with the others, we may now see how much we are contributing to the problems. Or, conversely, having assumed that we are to blame for difficulties, we may now see it is actually the other person who is driving much of the trouble. Our body is already rebalancing the one-sidedness of our conscious standpoint.

Having considered ourselves to be kind, considerate, and generous, we may suddenly run into a deep and willful, even arrogant and aggressive, narcissism within. Or having thought of ourselves as being shaky, confused, and without much to offer others, we may discover reservoirs of strength, confidence, and creativity that are quite unfamiliar. Perhaps we have always thought of ourselves as self-sufficient and confident, but we now uncover unsuspected levels of neediness and lack of confidence. If we are of the male gender, particularly of the older generation, we are likely to have been brought up to feel we have to be strong, independent, confident, and able to handle everything; in that case, coming upon deep levels of neediness, weakness, and even helplessness can be very challenging indeed. Or perhaps, if we have been brought up to identify with being unconfident, always dependent on others, and weak, positioning ourselves as the perpetual victim, the contrary information we are now receiving can be shocking and, while inspiring, equally difficult to handle. Again, the Soma is bringing us in touch with a fuller picture of who we actually are; it is beckoning us toward becoming whole. As you can imagine, when you are pursuing the somatic path, a lot of relationships have to be renegotiated, and not just once!

The more material that appears from the Soma, the more we find ourselves having to see, acknowledge, and take responsibility for being a much more complete and human person than we have thought and held ourselves to be. The ethical implications of the somatic work should already be clearly evident. From our ego standpoint, there is a lot of disquieting news here but, from another, larger point of view, it is wonderful to find ourselves gradually becoming so fully human, basically no different from anyone else.

None of this new information is arising without a point or a purpose. In fact, in what is breaking through from the unfathomable depths our Soma, we are correct to sense a kind of intention and agency. There is something behind what is going on here! In fact, all of the unexpected experiences and insights that appear out of the darkness of our body are expressions of our deepest Soma, our deepest person, our most fundamental Self.

What is wanted is that our conscious, ego mind align itself with the person we most deeply are and need to become, with the wholeness of person that our Soma embodies. In the unexpected manifestations of the somatic practices, we are being invited to follow the thread of our own journey; we are being shown the path to our own completeness, our basic uniqueness as a person and our own purpose for being at all. And this path must be shown to us moment by moment by our Soma, because there is no place of residence for it in our left brain, our conscious inventory of past experience that is made up only of abstract maps and facsimile versions. The Soma, our deepest Self, is all about the future fulfillment and completion of our life—and about what needs to happen right now to move us toward it.

So the smallest experiences and insights that emerge from our somatic practice are always about our person and our life in the largest possible perspective. Science now tells us that no electron moves without in some mysterious way reflecting the Totality of the universe, and so it is with us, even and especially into the depths of our most hidden, momentary, and elusive experiences. If we could fully comprehend the movement of that electron, we would comprehend, in an instant, the Totality. It is the same with our life: if we could be fully present to a moment of our life, we would see the whole. And, in fact, in the spiritual illumination of the body, sometimes that does occur.

1 4

How the Soma Protects Us and
Supports Our Transformation

As we are releasing tension and relaxing, and as we experience the steady influx of new information about ourselves and our lives, we may feel apprehension. We may feel that we have been ignoring a lot and so fear the arrival of new data that we can't handle; we might think that we will be inundated, flooded, and overwhelmed.

It is true that life and particularly a conscious, spiritually oriented life is always lived somewhat on the edge—on the edge of wondering whether or how we are going to be able to handle what comes up in the work. But my experience teaching the somatic work to thousands of people for the past thirty-five years suggests that fundamentally we can indeed relax and needn't worry overmuch. We are called to change in very basic ways, that is true. But we can remember that such changes are the heart and essence of the spiritual journey. They are about the fulfillment of our own human life; we are right on track. And it is an amazing and reassuring fact that in this process, the Soma protects, nourishes, and supports the basic changes and transformations we are going through. In particular, there seem to be two factors at work.

Becoming Anchored

The first is the grounding and stabilizing effect of the body work itself. The first two practices taught, Ten Points and Earth Descent, set the tone for all that follow. As we have seen, Ten Points brings us strongly into our body. And Earth Descent helps us to delocalize our awareness; lying down, opening the back of our body, so to speak, and extending our somatic scope down, down into the earth. Remember, the earth we are opening into is not quite the same as the one we have learned in geology. It is what we may call the experiential earth, the interoceptive earth, the reality that comes into view once we drop our concepts, extend our awareness downward, and see what we actually find in our experience.

Through this and other earth-related practices, over time we develop a strong, reliable, open, and profound relationship with the earth beneath us: a deep sense of the openness of the earth space, of its wonderful warmth and nourishment, and of ourselves being held and protected within it. My personal suspicion is that this experiential space is the same one we feel as fetuses in our mother's womb. The mother's womb *is* the earth in its microcosmic dimension; the earth *is* the womb of all that is. I tell my students, if you have unresolved issues with your mother and with inadequate maternal parenting, spend a lot of time in that earth space. The mother is the mediator of that fundamental cosmic reality; she is a human representative of the earth. So if you find yourself with unresolved wounds from your relationship with your mother, you can go back to the more profound, reliable, and timeless maternal space of the original womb. You will find the healing you seek there. This is something I learned from several of my indigenous teachers. While it may sound implausible or even outlandish, it is difficult to argue with the results.

Over time, we feel less and less isolated as a disconnected, physical entity running around on our barren, human parking lot; more and more we feel in connection, communication, and even communion with an alive, aware, sacred presence beneath us. This is always in need of emphasis: this is not an intellectual belief or conceptual understanding; rather it is something we feel in our body—and can only understand—with the corporeal, visceral intuition of the body. Once our body knows this presence, our whole state of being knows it directly, and this is the critical piece. Then we feel ourselves to be grounded, stabilized, and deeply rooted.

When we feel anchored in the earth in this primal way, then somehow the comings and goings of our ever-changing psychological states don't seem quite so weighty, momentous, or final. Trungpa Rinpoche, from whom I first heard this teaching, said we develop the direct and personal feeling of our Self, our body, as the mountain, anchored, rooted very deeply in the earth. As mentioned, all kinds of weather may come through, including storms with thunder and lightning, occasionally tornadoes. But in all of it, the mountain—our basic state of being—is as deep and stable as the earth herself, immovable and immensely peaceful—for, as we have seen, our basic state incarnated as our form is not separate from the earth. When we are thus grounded in the earth, we are able not only to tolerate but to accommodate and even eventually appreciate all the psychological weather that happens up here on the surface in our day-to-day life, and we are able to work with that turbulence in a most creative way.

Beyond Earth Descent, the other somatic protocols all carry forward in one way or another this stabilizing and grounding effect. The more aware we become of our body, the more we feel how it is always connecting in with the energy of the earth and participating in her reality and how it is, in fact, an aspect of the earth in human form. Again, this is not primarily an intellectual understanding, but something we feel somatically with the unique certainty of direct, unmediated, bodily knowledge. We grow into an awareness that our body, in and of itself, rooted within itself, is energetically at one with the earth; it is not separate. Feeling that we are grounded in the immovability and unconditional stillness of the earth promotes a tremendous feeling of openness, curiosity, and confidence in relation to whatever comes up in the somatic work as well as a sense of utter well-being and fathomless peace.

Being Held in Safety

The Soma protects and supports our unfolding spiritual process in a second way. There seems to be at work within us—within our Soma—a natural, I suspect inborn, modulating effect in terms of the volume and also the intensity of what the Soma brings up to us, to our attention. I can't necessarily explain or even claim to understand the process, but it seems to me that the Soma knows unerringly what the limits of our ego mind are, exactly how much we can handle, what our ego consciousness is capable of integrating at this time. When Levine advises us to "pendulate" in this kind of work, I believe what he is advising is not some kind of external and extraneous technique so much as encouraging us to tune in to and trust an inborn and accessible tendency of modulation already within the body itself. He is asking us to listen to the body and follow its call for modulation or pendulation.

Hence, in order to take advantage of this inbuilt somatic wisdom, we as a conscious, ego self, have an essential role to play. Whenever we are working with our body, or meditating, or working on our self-process in any way for that matter, we always need to be checking in with our body, to tap into its precise feeling and what it has to say. As we are practicing, the body will always be willing to show us: "You can go a little further now," "This is a little too much, back off a little," or "That is enough for today. Take a break." Sometimes the body will communicate "This issue is too much for you to handle alone; you need some additional help." Of course, the communication rarely comes in words like these; it most often arrives as an intuitive bodily sense. In the beginning, when something like this comes up, we may not know if it is our reliable and trustworthy body that is speaking or whether we are having just a random thought. After a while, though, you will develop the capacity to tell the difference: "This is my body" or "No, this is my ego, my monkey mind, trying to coopt the process."

I want to emphasize this point very strongly: we have to check in with our Soma and not allow our own ambitions and agendas, our fears or wishful thinking, to override what the body unerringly knows. People sometimes hear that certain forms of meditation practice are dangerous. I am always telling my students that the only way this or any other type of meditation is dangerous is if you don't listen to your body and just push ahead based on your personal, monomaniacal ambition. If you listen to your body, or take a break when you are not sure what it is saying, you will be as safe as if you were tenderly held in the pure and perfect safety of a loving mother's arms.

In addition, because the somatic journey can bring up so much and with such directness and intensity, I think for all of us—new practitioners and experienced meditators alike—it is essential to check in with others about our practice in some kind of regular way. This could be talking with a meditation teacher, a fellow practitioner, a somatic teacher, or a trusted therapist. During some of my most difficult periods, I did not have a therapist or anybody else to help me, and maybe there was some good in that because I had to figure things out for myself. But generally, I don't feel this kind of approach is necessarily desirable or even a good thing. In my larger path and in the paths of most of the people I have taught, in fact, off-and-on therapy of a resonant somatic type has proved invaluable.

Regarding therapy in the context of somatic practice, an issue for all of us is developing the ability to know when to rely on a therapist and when not to. Most of the somatic work can and must be done relying on one's own resources and standing on one's own feet, so to speak. Although, as I said above, there are times when resorting to a therapist can be necessary and helpful, a danger for us may be that we end up engaging in perpetual therapy not because we are in perpetual crisis but just because it is easier than having to work things out for ourselves. In this kind of situation, ongoing dependence on a therapist becomes a built-in reference point in our journey, and this can actually have the effect of weakening us and undermining our own confidence in our experience and process.

Again, the Soma—as our deeper, omniscient Self—*will* take us right up to the limit, but there should be no cause for alarm or panic in this. The spiritual classics help us here, showing us that this is how genuine spiritual practice seems to work: we come to the limit of what we can handle, we see to what is beyond, and we realize that our current ego is not up to it; it is ill-equipped to manage and control the larger reality. Sometimes this ego defeat may bring a dark night of the soul, a feeling of losing it, a sense of incapacity. We may find ourselves in a temporary depression that is quite heavy, or experience intense angst or anxiety. But *this ego death is not fundamentally to be feared.*

Especially, this kind of experience is often the decisive moment of change. What we are going through is not only wholesome but the precondition of our actually growing and developing further. What is now known to be true of teenagers in spades is also true of adults: without regular, ongoing dysregulation we actually cannot grow and reregulate into a more inclusive, integrated state of being. As adults and especially as spiritual journeyers, we actually *need* to "lose it" on a regular basis and fall apart in order to make room for the next step. Perpetually trying to hold it all together, which most of us do most of the time, is not helpful and leads to a state of spiritual paralysis.

The somatic journey I am showing you is all about making room for this most powerful of all human spiritual processes; and in this the Soma holds us securely and safely even as we feel we are plunging into the abyss of the unknown and sometimes disappearing into it and dissolving. Over time, we become familiar with the feel of when we are being pushed beyond our ego's realm of capability; because we have seen the process so many times, we are able to some extent to relax with it, take interest in it, and surrender. And then we can marvel at the rebirth that follows the death.

A little more on therapy, but now arguing another side of the case: my experience over the past thirty-five years suggests that the tasks and challenges implied by the journey of Somatic Meditation and by any authentic spirituality has a necessary precondition. We need to be psychologically and socially functional and "healthy" at a minimum level. Perhaps we have been diagnosed with—or feel we are suffering from—some kind of unstable or incapacitating mental condition; in that case, effective psychological or psychiatric treatment, healing, and an inner feeling of stability and confidence need to occur *before* we take up the tasks and inevitable challenges of the somatic journey or any serious spiritual or meditative practice.

1 5

Paradoxes of the Soma

In the preceding discussion, I have been speaking of the Soma in two somewhat distinct ways: both as our own most fundamental Self and, at the same time, as a true "other," something we experience as outside any known or familiar frame of reference. I have also expressed this paradox in the two seemingly rather different functions performed by the Soma: first, its purely mirror-like, omniscient quality, its ability to reflect with clarity and accuracy whatever is going on with us or in our experience of the outside (the Self); and second, in terms of its having some kind of intention toward us, as if the Soma were an agent wanting to communicate with us and to intervene in our life (the "other"). In both cases, I am referring to the body that we meet and experience from the inside when, using the various somatic protocols, we enter interoceptively into the interior of this psycho-physical incarnation of ours. How can what we experience as our most authentic Self also be, at the same time, often experienced as something so other?

The Soma as Other and as the Groundless Ground

These two functions reflect our experience in using the somatic protocols: sometimes the Soma feels like the most challenging, threatening alien of all; other times it seems like our deepest and most intimate companion, the abode of true wisdom, authentic connection, and our deepest, most authentic Self. How can both be true? Trungpa Rinpoche provides some clarification. He calls the direct unmediated experience of our body the "basic ground," because here is our own most personal, intimate, and direct experience that, subsequently, the ego mind builds on and takes as grist for its conceptualizing mill. The basic ground really is our own person at its deepest level, and we feel it as such.

But, paradoxically, our deepest Self isn't a solid, objectifiable entity; it is rather *a process of unfolding,* which, in its true aspect, is beyond thought or speech. This is why Rinpoche terms this basic ground "groundless."[1] Our deepest Self is always fluid, in motion and process, "impermanent" as the Buddha says. There is nothing in it that can provide a stable reference point, anything solid to build on or hide in. Such is our human condition that the one thing our ego is most threatened by and fears is the person that, at the deepest level, we actually are and subliminally know ourselves to be. Hence we have the paradox: the actual ground of our person and our life, our true Self, is experienced as ultimately other and sometimes even terrifying. The Soma we meet in Somatic Meditation is thus certainly very, very different from the relatively fixed and solid idea of the body that, for most of our life, we have been taking as our physical self.

Thus in relation to our conscious standpoint, the Soma *is* both Self and also ultimate "other." It is absolutely "for us," but it is also the one part of our reality that does not go along with our attempts to domesticate and reduce experience into the bounded, restricted, judgment-laden enclosure of our conscious, ego mind.

In this sense, the Soma is far more "other" than the so-called external world, which generally is mostly a projection of our ego mind; for what we think and know of the world "out there" is a highly selective and limited conceptualized version.

Dimensions of the Body

The Soma that we come to know in Somatic Meditation is different from our conventional ideas of our body in another way. When we enter the somatic practices, we are beginning with our notion of our body as contained within the envelope of our skin. As we progress through the protocols, however, we gain intimations that there may be more to it. In fact, as we learn to set aside our assumptions and preconceptions about our body and really look, we begin to sense that the envelope of our skin is an arbitrary boundary. And we begin to experience, within our delimited body but not bounded by it, a much more extensive somatic field. It is still our body—interoceptively it is the same experiential space— but we see there is much more to the experience of "our body" than we previously thought.

For example, we may begin to get an inkling that our Soma actually has no boundaries at all: that while we may try to restrain and limit our somatic scope, we are continually called to let go and open further and further. In ancient Chan and Zen, it is said that in meditation our practice is to abide fully and completely in this immediate body of ours; over time though, we begin to discover that "this body of ours" actually includes the external incarnation of the world around us, even up to the entire cosmos with all its realms of being. As always with these wonderful practicing traditions, what is being referred to here is not theory but rather possibilities of actual, personal experience. Of course, we know scientifically that our body is porous, infinitely receptive, and intimately connected with our entire environment, but it is quite another matter to discover this experientially, in our practice and in our own body.

When we hear about this vastness of our body—that it has no boundaries and that our Soma in fact includes the cosmic Totality of what is—we might suspect dissociation. But this is not a dissociated state; in fact, it is the opposite. The ego is the dissociated state. To awaken to the cosmic dimensions of our own body is to be, finally, fully, 100 percent present and embodied, because this is the actual situation of our incarnation. The more we attend to our Soma and the more fully we come into it, without judgment or conceptualization, the more we see what our body *actually* is: it is limitless. We feel grounded, rooted, and physically completely present; we feel fully embodied and absorbed in concrete, present reality in this way; and, when we arrive there, we find our Soma is this limitless, this infinitely inclusive, domain.

Jill Bolte Taylor, in her fascinating field notes of her experience after a massive left-hemisphere stroke, describes something similar. She tells us that, with her left-brain, thinking ego consciousness temporarily knocked out, "For the first time I felt truly at one with my body."[2] At the same time, she says: "I could no longer clearly discern the physical boundaries of where I began and where I ended . . . I no longer perceived myself as a whole object separate from everything. Instead I blended in with the space and flow around me."[3] "I had lost my left hemisphere consciousness containing my ego center and ability to see my *self* as a single and solid entity separate from you."[4] "Without the traditional sense of my personal boundaries, I felt that I was at one with the vastness of the universe."[5] "My soul was as big as the universe and frolicked with glee in a boundless sea."[6]

Far from being a dissociated state, Taylor's was deeply embodied and incarnate. As she describes it, what happened in her stroke was that her thinking, ego mind was off-line leaving only the "body's instinctive consciousness,"[7] what I am calling here our somatic awareness. While Taylor felt little or no investment in her restricted, personal life, the experience of her stroke involved no disconnection from life in its largest scope, no dissociation, just seeing life as much vaster than her left brain had thought: *"What a strange and amazing thing I am. What a bizarre living being I am. Life. I am life. . . . Here, in this form, I am a conscious mind and this body is the vehicle through which I am ALIVE!"*[8] She also says that part of her somatic awareness included the direct (not left-brain mediated) knowledge of other people, an incredible sensitivity to what was going on for them, including her caretakers when she could not think, speak, or even consciously process information; moreover, she saw how she was in intimate interconnection with the life and very fabric of the universe, including all its realms and inhabitants. Jill Bolte Taylor had finally met her body, her Soma, absent the usual mental interference, and her experience was deeply illuminating and liberating. Not surprisingly, as mentioned, it changed her life forever. This was a level and degree of embodiment within her Soma that most people never have the opportunity to experience. But it is the goal of the somatic practices to make that boundless bodily awareness the basis of our own everyday human existence.

1 6

What the Body Knows

As we shall see below, not only is the Soma's field of awareness apparently unlimited, but what it actually knows within that boundless field also seems to have no limit, either. In Chan and Zen, this is what is meant by knowing the "ten thousand things": "To study the Buddha Way is to know the self. To study the self is to forget the self. To forget the self is to be enlightened by the ten thousand things," says Dogen.[1]

In the illumination of a mind that is finally free, each moment of our human experience becomes transparent to all the realms of being and all those incarnations that inhabit them; we know the Totality. This teaching is illustrated in the description of "Indra's Net" found in the classical Mahayana sutra, the Avatamsaka, much loved in East Asian Buddhism. As the account goes, Indra, the creator of the universe according to Indian mythology, has brought about all that exists in the form of a vast net, all-inclusive and coextensive with the universe itself. At each cross-tie in this nearly infinite web there is a jewel. Each jewel represents each moment of our human experience when viewed without conceptual overlay or interference; in other words, what is there for us within the visceral range of the Soma. Each of these jewels is not only itself, this moment in space and time, but simultaneously, as part of its very nature, it also reflects all the other myriad jewels at all the other cross-ties throughout the entire cosmos. Hence, when we behold one jewel, we find reflected in it the Totality of Being. In beholding one jewel, this seemingly local and time-bound event, we find ourselves beholding Totality. This is precisely how and what the Soma knows.

William Blake refers to something similar when he talks about finding eternity in a grain of sand: the grain of sand is this present, timeless moment of experience; eternity is the Totality in its most boundless extent. More abstractly, in Indian Buddhism, this same experience is referred to as the omniscience (*sarvajna*) of Gautama Buddha. It doesn't mean that the Buddha is somehow the ultimate encyclopedia or database. It means that because his mind is completely open, his field of awareness is limitless; and because it is limitless, everything that is, is held, with knowing, within it. Again, this teaching is not philosophy; it is direct experience. This is what it means to know "things as they are"; it is this real, this concrete, and this vast. And it is this personal experience that liberates us and makes us free.

Not only can we can know the Totality of the cosmos in the most internal and subtlest experiences of Somatic Meditation, but in fact, our body is the only place where we can know that vast reality in a direct and fully experiential way.

Let me cite a few examples. Many people, both somatic practitioners and others, report experiences of "knowing" within the body that have occurred with visceral directness—thus without left-brain mediation—and for which they have no logical explanation. I go to an acupuncturist, a wise and wonderfully trained Chinese man from Taiwan, who has an accuracy that never ceases to astonish me. When I ask him, "How did you know that?" he replies, "I don't know how I know, I just know." Similarly, many of us have had the experiences of being with another person and intuitively knowing, actually directly feeling, what they are experiencing as if it were our own experience. How is this possible? Talking about "mirror neurons" merely associates this kind of experience with a particular part of our brain; it doesn't actually explain how our body is able to pick this up such information.

Indigenous peoples with totemic traditions talk about entering the state of being of their totem animal—say a hawk, a jaguar, or an eagle—and experientially becoming that animal, assimilating its knowledge, power, and unique life force. The Berserkers of ancient Scandinavia, so feared in battle by their enemies, would don wolf-skins (not armor) and then enter combat in a savage, trancelike fury that was, so it was believed, literally undefeatable. My teacher Mircea Eliade, in speaking about classical Indian yoga, once said that the yogin is, in essence, assimilating his state of being to that of a tree, entering into the stillness, the rootedness, and the incredibly slow process of a tree's way of being. How is such communion and identification with what is outside available to our Soma?

We find similar teachings in Chan and Zen. Ueda, in his article "Two Streams of Yogacara," cites the example of beholding a mountain, from the viewpoint of a Zen practitioner. Tracking an important Zen teaching, at first the mountain looks like an ordinary mountain. Then, as our awareness opens, we realize that all of our preconceptions and overlays—our left brain labeling and conceptualizing and interpreting—are irrelevant and we let them go. At that point, the mountain isn't a mountain; it isn't anything; it is "empty" of being a mountain. But then our awareness opens even further, and suddenly we see the mountain is *really* a mountain. Ueda explains: now we are seeing, we are experiencing, the mountain as it truly is and as it exists *from its own side*. "We are seeing the mountain as the mountain sees itself."[2] We are knowing tangibly and viscerally, from the side of the mountain's own experience of itself, what it is like to be a mountain. This is how our Soma knows; this is what our Soma knows.

Finally, and more close to hand, how are we to understand that, in opening into one of the many trackless inner regions of our body, we sometimes find ourselves lost in fathomless space, tasting an experience that seems best described in physics as the quantum emptiness of the beginning? Or how are we to make sense of the somatic perception of boundless and formless energy arising from that space, which, again, seems to have cosmological reverberations? Or, finally, as my students sometimes report, how can it happen in that vast and stupendous space, that we come upon stars and nebulae and galaxies in endless array? How can such experiences be? And yet they happen. It is not just that we *see* these things—the visual metaphor is inadequate—but that we sense them, we feel them from the inside. We feel, for an instant, what it is like to be them. For an instant we *are* them; they are us; this is who and what we are at this moment. Again far from disembodiment and dissociation, such experiences represent a level of embodiment, connection, and communion that few of us modern people have ever suspected possible. Such examples, puzzling as they may seem to our modern, logical minds, are not only quite real but are well-known to meditators, past and present. And, to reiterate, they liberate us into a state of being and an experience of freedom and joy for which, it now seems, we were born and for which we *are* at all.

I do not have, nor should I or can I have, any answers or explanations for how such things are possible, for, in a sense, they are not appropriately addressed by any possible explanation. They are, rather, not questions but statements of the ultimate mysteries of being. Still, with the reader's indulgence, I would like to muse with you about how we might begin to contemplate them.[3]

In the experience of somatically based meditation, when our conscious mind has opened to and identified with the somatic awareness of our body, one feels—perhaps you felt it in the Rooting practice—the body "light up." This is not an experience of this or that part or aspect of the body, but of the body as a whole.

We may have the strong impression that we are feeling down to a cellular level. It seems that we are sensing each cell in our body come awake, alive, and aware, or more precisely that we are connecting with the wakefulness, the abundant life, and the awareness that is already going on in our body and its cells. At this time, we may sense that each cell of the body is alert, receptive, feeling, and cognizant. When we talk about somatic awareness, this feels like ground zero, the baseline, the foundation: the knowingness of each cell.

Sciences such as biochemistry and neurobiology increasingly are suggesting that each of the cells of our body does in fact have its own integral state of being, its own form of consciousness, its own intention toward survival, its own emotions, its own knowledge of its immediate environment, and its own "desire" to be in relationship with other similar cells.[4] We don't know what consciousness or awareness (whether of the whole person or an individual cell), in and of itself, actually is; that is one of the ultimate riddles of contemporary science. But we know it is there and we know that cells have it.

So let's muse. These cells in our body (as indeed in the multicelled bodies of all members of the animal and vegetable kingdoms) group together through neural links into what we might call "communities of awareness"; they link with each other and share awareness and information with one another; in association with one another, their awareness thus becomes more inclusive and of a higher order, and their functioning becomes more differentiated and complex. Obviously we are not attributing to our cells anything like what we identify as the "conscious awareness" of our usual experience; it is, rather, a very different kind and order of awareness that we have begun to contact in our Soma.

These communities of somatic awareness, then, enter into relationship with other similar communities and form a larger, more inclusive, metacommunities and collectivities of awareness, information exchange, and functioning. And so it goes until we have the very extensive awareness and nearly infinitely complex functioning of the human being, comprising both conscious and unconscious, as a whole.

Let me suggest this way of putting it: to speak of somatic awareness is what the individual cells of our body, collectively and in communication, exchange, and communion with one another, know. Of course, our conscious mind is usually aware of only a miniscule fragment of what the body knows—as mentioned, only a few parts out of a million. And this is further reduced the more rigid and pathological our ego standpoint is. In a very real sense, then, each cell is directly or indirectly in touch with every other cell; in a certain sense, like Indra's net, it knows what every other cell knows, what every grouping of cells knows, and what the organism as a whole knows. Perhaps this is what we are getting at when we talk about the harmonious functioning of the human body as a unified organism; the different parts of ourselves are in touch, in communication and cooperation, even in communion with one another.

I have said that spiritual realization involves becoming fully and completely who we are; and further, that process involves entering into and finally identifying with our Soma. Now we can understand just how literally this may need to be taken. We are an incarnation of unbelievable, mind-boggling subtlety and complexity. Through some 36 trillion cells, the Soma receives the nearly infinite moments of experience, as is. To become completely who we are, we enter into and identify with the somatic awareness which is, literally, everything that every one of the 36 trillion cells in our body, in collaboration with every other cell, knows. Thus becoming aware of who we are means knowing, being in touch with, everything that is known in our psycho-somatic totality, moment by moment. How could "becoming who we truly are" involve anything less concrete, less embodied, or less inclusive?

This also gives us a new understanding of just how grounded, embodied, and literal is the realization of "things as they are," the ultimate goal of Buddhist meditation. "Things as they are" refers not to some abstract, generic, perhaps even vacant state; quite to the contrary, it refers to everything that every cell in our body uniquely knows, that "we" as the inclusive, integrated unique community of their life, receive into our—their collective—field of awareness. Things as they are is, then, nothing more or less than the bare facticity, the "first-order knowledge" (the direct perception of the Soma) of what our Soma receives and knows and shares throughout our entire being, without—at first—the additional step of "second-order knowledge" (the post-filtering, post-processing knowledge of our ego consciousness). This integrated, total field of awareness and functioning is what defines the ultimate possibilities of our awareness and experience as humans. And, as mentioned, it reflects and "captures" experientially the Totality of what is. In this, then, lies the universally sought experience of utter spiritual fulfillment.

But where does the awareness that is possible to us end? If our consciousness really is stripped of all artificial barriers, is there any reason why our resulting awareness could not be infinitely sensitive and cognizant? Meditation experience suggests that this may well be so. So mightn't it be that each of our cells is an open and porous field of experience, with no inherent limit, receiving myriad, infinite—and sometimes infinitely subtle—forms of input from inside and outside our conventionally conceived body? If so, why wouldn't this input be all-inclusive—biological, energetic, cognitive, electromagnetic, and so on, including even cosmic microwave background radiation deriving from the very origins of the universe itself, as well as the dark energy and dark matter that are now suspected to run in all-pervasive patterns and fields throughout the entire universe?

1 7

Making Sense of Ego and Soma

A nother outcome of the Somatic Meditation protocols is a more nuanced view of the "mind-body relationship"—or in our terms, the relationship between the left-brain/thinking mind and the Soma. As mentioned, particularly in modern societies, there is a tendency for the left-brain, ego mind to function in a way that can only be described as pathological—that is, overly rigid, disconnected from the body, solipsistic, dysfunctional, and ill. In this, its linear, logical, linguistic style resists the Soma; and more, it dominates, marginalizes, and denies what somatic consciousness knows. If we are historians, we may want to trace this pathological development back to the rise of agriculture and the more and more complex societies it brought, where left-brain function increasingly became the most important adaptive function favoring survival.

When the left brain and the Soma are not communicating, the ego mind operates in relative isolation from the Soma. Then it is able to develop a logic that is relatively self-enclosed and self-convincing of the idea that things could not possibly be other than what it thinks. As McGilchrist explains, it takes its own concepts as reality itself, even when, as recent experimentation has shown, contrary information is present to the Soma's perceptual field. Smug "denial" in the face of overwhelming somatic evidence to the contrary seems to be one of the pathological ego's special skills.[1]

Often amid considerable distress, through the gritty, hands-on, somatic protocols, one comes to a direct and sometimes disturbing perception of the pathological ego as it functions in one's own life and experience. The somatic practices described above serve to expose the left-brain pathology. When this happens, when we begin to observe our left brain functioning from within the larger awareness of the body, the authoritative, dictatorial, self-certainty of our thinking mind begins to seem artificial, forced, and even nauseating. We are no longer able to believe unquestioningly what we think. Thus begins the process of dismantling the isolated ego; in the process, we begin to make more room for the unique reality and far more inclusive and accurate knowingness of the Soma.

At the same time, as we work our way through the protocols and their phases, we begin to notice another option for our ego, our conscious self: we see the possibility of the left-brain, ego mind operating in a nonpathological manner, a not-quite-so-linear way, in increasingly intimate connection with the Soma. The protocols bring this about by establishing links of communication—growing new neurons, neural fibers, neurological connections—between the direct experience of our Soma and the left hemisphere. As this happens, we see that our left-brain, ego mind does not disappear; instead, it begins to feel more wholesome and healthy, more realistic, connected, and grounded. At this point, our ego mind is becoming increasingly transparent to the new information that is constantly arising from the Soma, from the darkness of the un-conscious. Many indigenous peoples—relying on symbolic and ritual processes—do exhibit this kind of collaborative relationship between conscious mind and Soma, and one suspects that in the course of human evolution the distinct yet functional relationship between the conscious and unconscious, the ego and Soma, was likely the original state of affairs.

As new information comes in, we are able to "update our files," in Jill Bolte Taylor's metaphor, and delete those files that are out of date. The healthy ego consciousness is thus receptive to—and nourished and reinvigorated by—the continual influx of new data; and it is able to change its point of view, as needed, in an ongoing way. The ego consciousness is then open and malleable; it is fluid and flexible; it is able to let go of ideas, preconceptions, and beliefs that no longer apply and reform conceptual pictures, the maps, that are more apt and appropriate to reality as it is showing itself, right now.

Seen from the standpoint of Somatic Meditation, the ego has two primary functions: first, a self-imaging function, and, second, a managerial function. In terms of the self-imaging function, our conscious mind is continually engaged in the process of defining and redefining—and protecting and maintaining—our identity: who we think ourselves to be now in relation to what we think of as our world and who we think ourselves to be over the course of our life (our story). This has the potential to be an entirely healthy and creative human process. The managerial function puts into operation and actualizes in our life the intentions, plans, and agendas arising from our self-imaging function.

When the self-imaging function is pathological, it is forming and reforming our conceptual identity in isolation, in ignorance of and often contradiction to our actual experience and in opposition to the facticity of our life and world—as directly and unerringly known by our Soma. When this happens, then the managerial function is in the service of this pathology and serves to prop it up and reinforce it. By contrast, when the self-imaging function is operating in a wholesome way, through its transparency to the Soma and constant updates based on somatic data, then the managerial function acts as a reflection of and in support of our healthy self-imaging.

Somatic Meditation shows us a way through which, by entering through the gate of the Soma, we can heal our dysfunctional, pathological ego. From one point of view, the process could not be simpler. When, through somatically grounded meditation practices, we turn our attention to our Soma, we are already healing the neurological and cognitive breach between left brain and Soma. The more we attend to our Soma, the more we are able to tune in to its own style of awareness. And the more we tune in to this, the more we are able to unlock the inborn, natural tendency of the mind to heal itself.

1 8

Changes in Our Ongoing
Relationship with Our Body

S omatic Meditation brings us face-to-face with what is left when we descend beneath the conceptualizing, pigeonholing, filtering ego mind. And what is left, we discover, is pretty much everything in the way of naked experience. What we meet in our Soma is the concrete experience of our life as it *actually is* before we think about it, before we reduce it, label it, and judge it. We come upon a realm that is open and endless, that is alive with energy and dynamism, that is uncertain, exciting, and free. And we discover that, ultimately, this is *really us* underneath all the rampant thinking; it's fundamentally who we are in all our fullness and mystery. This is a realm most of us have rarely or never experienced or even touched in a pure way, and for some of us, it can be quite shocking.

The more we come into direct contact with our factual—as opposed to conceptualized—body, the more we begin to see how much of our incessant thinking process is actually an impulsive reactivity away from the groundless ground of our actual Soma— where we run away from the openness and intense energy of our direct experience into the safer, more secure and predictable world of thoughts and concepts about how everything is or should be. Thus, through the somatic protocols, we begin to become sensitized to the difference between thinking, on the one hand, and direct experience, on the other—a distinction that will become increasingly important as our practice with the body unfolds.

As we work our way through the protocols, we gradually uncover in our body an experience of relaxation, peace, and unencumbered ease. By allowing the body to release its tension and the secrets it holds, relieved of the oppositional behavior of ego, the whole body is finally able to settle, open, and fall into a profound stillness. Sometimes this experience can be dramatic indeed: where no matter where we look, there are no thoughts or disabling feelings, just the infinite space of being itself. For many of us, this discovery may come as a profound, even ecstatic, spiritual opening.

As we carry forward with our somatic practice, we begin to include this new, larger awareness as part of our ongoing way of feeling about ourselves and about being at home in our body and in the world. We become sensitive to the livingness of our body. It is dynamic, ever changing, and filled with energy and life. The body becomes a revelation in and of itself, independent and outside of any interpretive framework—religious, psychological, or otherwise.

As we practice, we become more and more sensitive to our own wayward tendencies. More than ever, we feel the impact when we turn away from our body though discursive thinking—we become numb, tense, feel that we've lost our ground. Because we've had the experience of the simplicity and directness of our bodily life, purely conceptual experience doesn't feel right anymore. In fact, it can feel not only completely unsatisfying, but unbearable. When that occurs, we discover that we can actually best address this situation by coming back to our somatic beingness; we are learning how to heal our self or, rather, how our body, given room, heals us. We begin to experience a state of being that is embodied, visceral, grounded, open, and always in process, and we begin to feel that this is our authentic person and the life we were put on this planet to live.

When we experience something without jumping immediately to conclusions, to categorizing, evaluating, and judging, we begin to discover the realm of pure experience: an approaching storm is portentous, filled with its own impending power that we can sense in our body, that saturates our feeling with its own being, its own meaning, its "isness." And we are brought into a state of utter stillness and awe before it. We smell it, we taste it, and we receive it into our being. Nothing need, should, or can be done in addition, so overwhelming, so final—and sacred, really—is its stark reality.

And so it may be with everything else we encounter in our life. We realize that there's a certain fundamental raw and naked and rugged reality to things we have never experienced in quite this way, that we never even realized was there. And so we gradually discover in ourselves a larger, vaster range of emotional and perceptual experience than we have ever previously known or even suspected. We begin to sense the limitless terrain of our somatic being—the endless, open spaces we can enter through the body and the seemingly infinite scope of experience that arises from that. Now we have an approach, a method, a context within which we can actually experience the full possibilities of this endless, mysterious physical incarnation of ours.

PART FOUR

Final Thoughts

19

The Soma and Our Human Genome

Birth, maturation, completion, and death are characteristic of all of life. There is a life cycle that every living being goes through, whether that being is an oak tree, a one-celled animal, the birds and the fish, all the four-leggeds, and also humans. But the life cycle also includes every manifestation, every phenomenon, everything that is. There is a beer commercial here in Colorado that says, in effect, "Mountains are on their own journey. They take plenty of time on their way. That's how we like to make beer, long and slow." Whether you like beer or not, the commercial makes an important point: everything has its life and everything is making its own journey.

Until relatively recently, physicists believed that although everything else may have its own life cycle, the universe itself is the one big exception. In the early twentieth century, Albert Einstein himself initially believed that the universe was ever and always the same; it never basically changed; its inner dynamic occurred within a fixed frame of reference. Even when his equations showed this was not the case, Einstein resisted. The British astronomer

Fred Hoyle championed the same point of view. It was only when mounting, incontrovertible experimental evidence, beginning with the direct observations of Edwin Hubble, showed this not to be the case that the dike of a changeless universe gave way. Now we accept that even the entire universe itself, both the seen and the unseen, is making a journey; all manifest reality is, in fact, an organic whole with birth, maturation, completion, and death. (Brian Swimme writes beautifully about this in his 2011 book, *Journey of the Universe*.)

We now know that the life cycle of us humans is encoded and fully present within our human genome (the name given to the totality of the genetic inheritance of our species). It includes the complete set of the nucleic acid sequence for humans, encoded as DNA within the twenty-three chromosome pairs in our cells. Every stage in our development—from the first moment when egg and sperm unite, through birth, infancy, childhood, adolescence, adulthood, aging, and death—is encoded in our genome. The genome evidently contains the predispositions for many things that we once thought we purely cultural, including language.

My own suspicion is that what we call "spirituality"—as a predisposition and a capacity—is also encoded within our genome, traceable back to the original community of *Homo sapiens* in northern Africa. As a historian of religion, I ask myself, how else can we explain the extraordinary continuities and parallels in the shape and character (though not the content) of human spirituality across time and space?

Current neurobiological research offers a provocative datum about this. We know that as adults age and approach death, some aspects of their previous mental functioning tend to recede, such as the left-brain analytic capacities to calculate numbers quickly, skill at crossword puzzles, ease with preparing their income taxes, and so on. At the same time, other capacities are growing and developing, including the ability to pay attention to a much wider field of experience; an increase in openness toward experience and the world; a capacity to attend to the larger world in a more unbiased and objective way, not so tangled in personal subjectivity; an increased empathy toward the value and worth in those very different from ourselves; and a more and more broad acceptance of what life, and especially their own life, has been. None of this heralds dejected resignation but rather indicates an increase in qualities that—truth be told—cultures have always identified as spiritual maturation and even realization. And, the evidence suggests, it is right there in the genetic map for our human life cycle in the inborn evolution of the human brain approaching death.

It has often been observed that we humans are unusual (if not unique) in our special capacity to obstruct and even derail the inherent, natural life cycle that is part of our genetic inheritance. Many psychologists, sociologists, and anthropologists, beginning in the second half of the last century, have suggested that our sociocultural conditioning often lays down in us highly compromised patterns of thinking about ourselves and our world and leaves us unable to grow. We can easily observe that many people in modern societies, in terms of their emotional development, never get out of adolescence. Few and far between, today, are the people who, as they approach the end of life, are able to grow unobstructedly into the full understanding, wisdom, empathy, and acceptance that appears to have been far more prevalent in past human societies.

The primary culprit, I believe, is the extraordinary disembodiment that we all suffer from today and, as a result, the excessive, even extreme investment each one of us has in left-brain pictures of reality—including pictures of ourselves, others, and the world. The mental constructs of our thinking mind are, by their nature, not only incomplete and biased, they are incompetent; when we hang on to them, and keep repeating to ourselves their twisted rationalizations and justifications, they poison not just our families and our societies, but our entire lives and our world. Pernicious and virulent beyond question, our left-brain addictions and obsessions cut us off, sometimes completely, from the direct, nonconceptual experience of our body, from the naked and life-giving realities of our Soma.

Only the direct, limitless eventfulness of the Soma can enable the ever-flowing river of our genome to proceed along its natural course. In Somatic Meditation we are tapping into the deepest and most integral life of our body. As we have seen in the practice, our left brain, with all its obstructions, its obfuscations, and its deadening effect, temporarily goes off-line. Then we find ourselves aligned with our own fundamental, somatic human process; we are aligned with the direction and momentum of our human genome. We are not just moving in the direction of greater life; we ourselves have become an expression of that greater life and we can feel it.

When we practice Somatic Meditation, then, we are calling fully into action the journey of our genome and aligning ourselves with it; we are making room for the unfolding of the life stages that are inborn within us, through adulthood, to the spiritual realization that is always out there, calling from the depths.

20

The Soma and the Cosmos

One of the core and most important teachings of Somatic Meditation is that our human body is a microcosm of the universe, the macrocosm. This means, in effect, that the cosmos in its unknowable, perhaps infinite extent is present and embodied—and, most importantly, experientially available—in our human form. When we think about this statement, we might have the impression that the universe is the real thing, the actual reality, while the body is a kind of miniature reflection or representation. It would be natural to assume, further, that our body is a kind of abridged and simplified version of the bigger thing. After all, how could the vastness, the complexity, and the full reality of the external universe possibly be completely present in our body? In other words, how could our Soma and the Totality of the cosmos possibly be just two different scales of exactly the same reality?

And yet, astoundingly, within the Asian somatic lineages, this is just what is being said: whatever the Totality of all of Being is, all of that is present and accessible in our human body. And, to emphasize, what is proposed is that we are not talking here about just the general outlines and overall reality of the universe; we are talking about its actual tangible facticity in all of its potential detail, complexity, and functioning.

Let us reflect briefly on this rather implausible possibility. As we have seen, the deeper we enter into the body, the more open and endless its awareness turns out to be and the more infinite the variety of the experience it holds. You have perhaps already glimpsed just how fathomless this interoceptive experience can be. As you have perhaps apprehended, you don't have to go very far into the somatic protocols to find yourself not in any circumscribed body or circumscribed anything at all, but hanging out with, within, and even *as* the cosmic Totality. Experientially, it would be more accurate to say you have arrived at an experience of reality that cannot be identified as "inside" or "outside" and that is endless in its extent: it has no perceivable limits, either those of space or those of time. Notions of here or somewhere else, then or now, simply do not apply to the actual experience. Please note: we are not talking here about some generic "timeless present" empty of content. The experience of the body as the Totality is, in every instance, highly specific and detailed.

Physicists, both those focusing on the micro-world of small particles and those looking primarily at the macro, cosmic entirety, are presenting us with a picture of the universe that is exciting, often startling, and deeply inspiring. Empty space gave birth to the energy of the beginnings and this is still a moment-to-moment occurrence, with the tiniest particles continually flashing into and out of existence within the quantum void. Energy and matter are two forms of the same thing; when you get right down to it, matter isn't solid but a kind of dense energy and, ultimately, is empty of any solidity or fixity at all. Time and space are not definite realities but depend on where you are standing and what you are doing. Reality is not local; events happening in one part of the universe are simultaneously creating repercussions billions of light years away. Past, present, and future are likely constructs that we put on an observable reality that seems to be far more undifferentiated. And on and on it goes.

In an intriguing sense, as we have seen, what contemporary physics is discovering and what we find out through Somatic Meditation often seem to be running along parallel lines. Both are empirical in their approach and experimental in their attitude.

Unlike other forms of meditation, Vajrayana is intensely interested in how experience—the relative experience of conditioned reality—manifests and how it works all within the "uncultivated field" of emptiness. As always, we are talking here about something interoceptive, the direct, nonconceptual experience that we discover within our Soma. And touching and learning how to bathe in the vastness is only the first step, only the beginning of the journey, as the somatic teachers say. After that, comes our engagement with the relative reality of our naked experience, our exploration, the immense discoveries, witnessing its cycles of birth, death, rebirth, and, in Trungpa Rinpoche's words, the ongoing "journey without goal." We can identify all of these somatic themes and inspirations in the way contemporary physics describes the universe.

However, one critical difference between contemporary physics and Vajrayana is all important. Contemporary physics assembles a picture of the whole that is essentially conceptual, from the insights gained from theoretical and mathematical thinking in collaboration with evidence derived from experimental research. In the case of physics, the collaboration is deep: theoretical models can suggest directions for experimentation; and experimentation can then verify, discredit, or alter the direction of further theorizing.

In Vajrayana, the "picture" of the Totality arises as an immediate, spontaneous, nonconceptual apprehension of the whole. And this apprehension is directly perceived to be outside of both temporal and spatial coordinates, all the while it includes them. For somatic spirituality, until we know incarnate reality in this way, we do not know it at all. To know the Soma as it truly is, is to know the Totality of Being itself. Indra's net. And to arrive here is to be free.

For this reason, according to Vajrayana, we are able to know the Totality directly only in and through the body, the only place where direct, nonconceptual experience occurs. What we may know of the universe conceptually takes second place. This point of view is beautifully articulated in Taoist spirituality and one finds it implicitly in both Chan and Zen. Mental pictures of the universe must always be indirect, partial, and biased because they are constructed out of abstractions from experience itself. Vajrayana teachings suggest that mental pictures cannot liberate us from the trammels of our suffering; only direct experience can.

I sense, though, that the relationship between modern physicists and Vajrayana practitioners may be more nuanced. Reading the personal accounts of modern physicists, it is undeniable that for many, the discipline of physics is a spiritual endeavor. The great discoveries (and the small ones) transform those who make them and those who behold them. Look at the avidity with which so many of us follow scientific findings; some people would rather read astronomy magazines than do almost anything else. The passion and self-sacrifice involved in modern physics cannot be explained if what is at stake there is only a more accurate understanding of the external world. I suspect that the same can be said of all the sciences.

Perhaps what makes scientific discoveries so deeply significant, meaningful, and impactful for so many is that they are not only laying bare the macrocosm, they are also disclosing the microcosm, the deepest, most intimate domains of our personal human experience. From the somatic point of view this would make sense, because the outer world and the inner world are actually the same reality and you can access either through the other. So now I must revise my statement that modern physics knows only conceptually, from the outside; I think in a certain way it opens a kind of experiential window into the reality that transcends outside and inside.

For the somatic lineage, the discoveries of small-particle physics and astrophysics can be tremendously inspiring, reassuring, and incentivizing. Tibetan texts rarely speak, at least in language that is readily accessible to a modern reader, about the full measure of what happens on the somatic path. Thus it is that when you approach meditation as a somatic practitioner, many things occur for which there appears to be no language in the texts or the commentaries. But reading in modern astrophysics and cosmology, surprisingly, you find very precise language given to what you are finding out every day on your meditation cushion. You come face-to-face with some kind of ultimate space, beyond any ordinary experience of space, and you discover that time does not really exist in the depths. Continually, you may find yourself at the moment of nothing (quantum emptiness) and then something, some primal manifestation that arises out of that vacuity, and the process is far beyond any recognition or naming. And then, in a process of "cooling," that primordial energy begins to take more recognizable shape and finally becomes seemingly solid in our ego process.

It is entirely mysterious and deeply compelling: we seem to abide in two worlds at once, the relative world of all of our experience without exception and the realm of quantum emptiness where completely different rules apply, where all of our experience is grounded and from which all of it arises. And perhaps this is the ultimate realization of somatic spirituality, what it means to be fully embodied: to find oneself present to the entirety of what it means to be human and to identify with a reality and a process that stands not only beyond our own life and death, but, at the same time, beyond the life and death of the universe itself.

LIST OF AUDIO TRACKS

Audio recordings of the six guided meditations introduced in this book are available for free download online at www.shambhala.com/theawakeningbody.

1. Practice One: Ten Points
2. Practice Two: Earth Descent
3. Practice Three: Yin Breathing
4. Practice Four: Coming into the Central Channel
5. Practice Five: Whole Body Breathing and Rooting
6. Practice Six: Twelvefold Lower-Belly Breathing

NOTES

CHAPTER 1. Somatic Meditation

1. Quoted from Khenpo Tsultrim Gyamtso, teachings on Thogel, restricted transcript. Vajravairochana Translation Committee, 1996, 1997, 1998.

CHAPTER 3. Consider Your Body's Mind

1. Louis Cozolino, *The Neuroscience of Human Relationships* (New York: W. W. Norton & Company, 2006) 25.
2. Jill Bolte Taylor, *My Stroke of Insight: A Brain Scientist's Personal Journey* (New York: Viking, 2008), 33.
3. Cozolino, *The Neuroscience of Human Relationships,* 25.
4. Taylor, *My Stroke of Insight,* 29.
5. Ibid., 139.
6. Ibid., 29, 49.
7. Ibid. Taylor's description of the state of mind of the right brain can intuitively be connected with Buddhist "nirvana."

In Buddhism, it is the right brain that is the seat of the experience of the "buddha mind," the "buddha nature" and the experience of "buddha *jnana*"—that is, the "wisdom of a buddha" or what a buddha knows.

CHAPTER 7. Practice Three: Yin Breathing

1. Kristofer M. Schipper, *The Taoist Body* (Berkeley and Los Angeles: University of California Press, 1993) 103–108.
2. N. J. Giardot, *Myth and Meaning in Early Taoism: The Theme of Chaos* (Berkeley and Los Angeles: University of California Press, 1974).

CHAPTER 8. Practice Four: Coming into the Central Channel

1. Taigen Dan Leighton, *Cultivating the Empty Field: The Silent Illumination of Zen Master Hongzhi* (North Clarendon: Tuttle, 2000) 46, 47.

CHAPTER 9. Practice Five: Whole Body Breathing and Rooting

1. Readers who have practiced "cellular breathing" as found in my 2008 audio course *Your Breathing Body* and other past recorded programs will notice that the version offered here is somewhat different from those iterations, being more gentle, slow-moving, and less effortful.
2. Candace B. Pert, *Molecules of Emotion: The Science Behind Mind-Body Medicine* (New York: Touchstone, 1999).

CHAPTER 12. Tension and Breathing

1. This teaching reflects an important Dzogchen view, taught by Chögyam Trungpa, that our separated human self-consciousness is merely a fragment of our basic awareness that has split off and sequestered itself as an apparently different reality. Through the practice of meditation, this

fragmented awareness may be returned and reintegrated into the totality of awareness from which it came in the first place.

2. Thanissaro Bhikkhu trans., "Bāhiya Sutta: Bāhiya" (Ud 1.10), *Access to Insight (Legacy Edition)*, 3 September 2012, http://www.accesstoinsight.org/tipitaka/kn/ud/ud.1.10.than.html.

CHAPTER 15. Paradoxes of the Soma

1. See Chögyam Trungpa, *Cutting Through Spiritual Materialism* (Boston: Shambhala Publications, 2002) 122–23. See also Chögyam Trungpa, *Orderly Chaos: The Mandala Principle* (Boston: Shambhala Publications, 1991) 95–105.

2. Taylor, *My Stroke of Insight*, 43.

3. Ibid., 41.

4. Ibid., 74.

5. Ibid., 67.

6. Ibid., 71.

7. Ibid., 141.

8. Ibid., 42.

CHAPTER 16. What the Body Knows

1. More fully, from the *Genjōkōan*:

> To study the Buddha Way is to study the self. To study the self is to forget the self. To forget the self is to be enlightened by the ten thousand things. To be enlightened by the ten thousand things is to drop off body and mind of self and other. No trace of enlightenment remains, and this traceless enlightenment continues endlessly.

Kazuaki Tanahashi and John Daido Loori trans., *The True Dharma Eye: Zen Master Dōgen's Three Hundred Kōans* (Boston: Shambhala Publications, 2005), xlix.

2. Yoshifumi Ueda, "Two Streams of Yogacara," *Philosophy East and West, vol. 17* (Hawaii: University of Hawaii Press, 1967) 164–165.

3. In what follows, I write as an entirely uninformed layperson. What I want to do here is to use some themes that are abroad in the culture, as metaphors or even just starting points, to think about how the body might come to know reality in a total, unique way and to the limitless extent that it does.

4. Candace Pert in her work on the molecules of emotion doesn't go nearly this far, but to me this is what her work suggests as distinct possibility.

CHAPTER 17.   Making Sense of Ego and Soma

1. Iain McGilchrist, *The Master and His Emissary: The Divided Brain and the Making of the Western World* (New Haven: Yale University Press, 2009) 32, 66.

INDEX